EASY RICHES

EASY RICHES

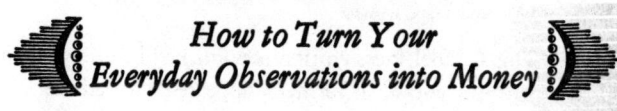

*How to Turn Your
Everyday Observations into Money*

TOM TAYLOR

Citadel Press   Secaucus, New Jersey

Copyright © 1982 by Tom Taylor
All rights reserved.

Published by Citadel Press
A division of Lyle Stuart Inc.
120 Enterprise Ave., Secaucus, N.J. 07094
In Canada: Musson Book Company
A division of General Publishing Co. Limited
Don Mills, Ontario

This Citadel Press edition is published by arrangement with the author. It formerly appeared entitled *Get Rich on the Obvious* (1982) from Harcourt Brace Jovanovich, Publishers.

The author wishes to thank the following for permission to quote from the sources given: *Barron's,* words from Alan Abelson's column; *Forbes* Magazine, a January 1981 article by Newcomb Stillwell; *The Wall Street Journal,* "The Coming Revolution in World Oil Markets," S. Fred Singer, © Dow Jones & Company, Inc. 1981, and "Economists Don't Share Granville Market View," © Dow Jones & Company, Inc. 1981.

Manufactured in the United States of America

ISBN 0-8065-1029-3

*To Peggy, my wife and coauthor,
whose work and support made it happen*

Special thanks go to fellow stockbroker Richard Vance for his input and contribution to detail.

Thanks also to Percy Williams for all the final typing and editing, and to Julie Olfe for the copy editing. In addition, much appreciation goes to my secretary, Christine Mayer, and to fellow stockbroker Raymond Smith.

CONTENTS

Introduction 3

1. 100% Schwartz 7

2. Using Open-Air Analysis to Pick Bottoms 13

3. How to Make Money Through the Use of Open-Air Analysis 33

4. Open-Air Analysis versus Other Market Approaches 49

5. My Broker Made Me Do It 66
(Are Brokers Worth It?)

6. Can Your Stockbroker Find Happiness with Open-Air? 77
(Does the Commission System Work Against Your Profits?)

7. The Client 95

8. Stockmarket Winners or Losers Test 107
(Maybe You Should Stay in a Passbook Savings Account)

9. When to Fire Your Broker 128

10. When a Client May Be Fired 141

11. Tips on Managing Your Portfolio 157
(Does It Ever Pay to Panic?)

12. Joe Granville and the Institutions 175
(Can Open-Air Beat Those Guys?)

13. Open-Air Analysis Looks at Profits in the Eighties 186
(What Might Be Obvious in 1982 and 1983)

Index 211

EASY RICHES

INTRODUCTION

Most of us are so busy analyzing the obscure that we miss the obvious. Worse yet, when we finally recognize the obvious we never consider the possibility that we can make money on it.

In the spring of 1978, several people simultaneously approached a new device that had been installed on the outside wall of their local bank. The device was an automatic teller machine made by Diebold. "What won't they think of next!" said one man. "Helps me plan my weekends better," replied another. One observant woman asked, "Who's the manufacturer?" The woman went to see her broker with the question "What do you know about a company called Diebold?"

As a result of her recognition of the obvious and the subsequent discussion with her broker, she invested $10,000 in Diebold in the spring of 1978; in the spring of 1981 it was worth $40,000.

That's what this book is about—converting your everyday observations into profits in the stock market. I call it Open-Air Analysis, and it is the secret to success. Some call it common sense; others call it vision; but I call it Open-Air because most observations that can make you rich hit you in the "open air" and not in the office. But analysis and screening are required. That's where your broker can either help you get rich on the obvious or, by his actions, help you eliminate stocks as an investment choice.

That is why I wrote this book! If the definition of an expert is one who has made the most mistakes, then I'm an expert. As a stockbroker for twenty-four years (interrupted for several years when I cofounded my own financial services firm), I have shared frustration with fellow brokers over the inability of most people to make a lot of money in the stock market. If only they knew how to use Open-Air Analysis!

I never thought about making a million dollars until I became a broker, in 1958. Then I realized it could be done. One of my first obvious Open-Air experiences was with Stouffer Foods in 1960. After several trips to the supermarket, I began to observe those orange-and-black-packaged foods gathering more and more shelf space. Finally, I asked the store manager, "What's going on with Stouffer Foods?" He told me it was his hottest-selling item. I came back to the office, checked the company out, and doubled my money in about six months. It was then I decided that I was going to be worth a million by the age of forty. By 1972 and at the age of forty-two, I had made it. At age forty-four, I had lost it all.

So there's that expert for you—familiarity with both sides of an equation. What is more revealing is that when I tell people this story, ninety-five out of a hundred ask me how I *lost* it. Maybe that's why fewer than 5% of the people ever get rich at anything. Winners are fascinated with tales of winning; losers are preoccupied with stories of losing.

I talk about winners and losers later in this book, but the big winners I have seen in the stock market all have one thing in common—they believe they can make money; they believe in the market; they believe in their brokers; they trust their own judgment, and they practice, practice, practice.

"How do you know when you've spotted a winner?" . . . "Well, what's obvious to you might not be obvious to me." These are legitimate challenges to Open-Air Analysis. This book will answer those questions. Most of us do not trust our own judgment. When it comes to making money, we feel others are better educated or possess finer analytical skills. If security analysis were the answer, all the analysts and stockbrokers would be rich. If understanding balance sheets and income statements were the answer, all the CPAs would be rich. If inside information were the answer, all corporate executives would be rich.

The answer is really a combination of all of the above, but it starts with Open-Air because that's what winners instinctively recognize and act upon. It is not difficult to learn Open-Air Analysis. Open-Air has only two prerequisites:

1. The ability to observe
2. The confidence to act

If you are going to convert your observations of the world around you into profits in the stock market, you've got to get in shape, and you must find the right broker. For a country that believes in getting in shape physically, I propose that we get in shape by recognizing the obvious. After you have read this book, your "get rich" reflexes will be fine tuned. As you hear news items, observe new products, or detect changes in lifestyles, your Open-Air response will be automatic.

This book is written as it was lived by a stockbroker, from early 1980 through the spring of 1981—a period referred to as "from Bunker Hunt day through Joe Granville day to attempted-assassination day." It was a period beset by one of the most severe stock market plunges in history, hostages held in Iran, Russia's invasion of Afghanistan, the

uncertainty of an election, a new president with radical new ideas, and finally an attempt on President Reagan's life. The point is—stock markets always have uncertainties, but Open-Air does not depend on political climate, business environment, economics, or stock market direction. In good or bad markets, the individual practicing Open-Air makes money.
YOU'LL SEE!

100% SCHWARTZ

In the spring of 1979, when you were sitting in those gas lines, did it occur to you to buy an oil stock?

It was not very obvious then that $10,000 invested in the stock of a young oil company called Tom Brown was going to be worth $112,000 by the end of 1980. But it might have been obvious in the spring of 1979 that investing $10,000 in Texaco, Standard Oil of California, Standard Oil of Indiana, and Gulf would be a very smart move. It was. The results at the end of 1980:

Texaco	$20,000
Standard Oil of California	$22,700
Standard Oil of Indiana	$30,000
Gulf Oil	$20,000

One good investment is worth a lifetime of hard work. Most of us miss it. It's not because of the money, and it's not because of courage—it's because we don't recognize the opportunity. Or worse, when we finally realize what's going on, it's too late. Others get rich and we only get frustrated. This book will awaken your money-making senses and, as a result, some of you will get rich.

How do you get rich on the obvious? By using the technique called Open-Air Analysis. It is the ability to convert your awareness of your environment into profits in the stock market—a commonsense approach that transcends the mystery of security analysis. You can make money on fundamental analysis, and you can make money on technical analysis, but you can get *rich* on Open-Air Analysis.

It was not very obvious that a person could put $10,000 into the stock of Teledyne on its low of January 1976 and have it worth $154,000 by the end of 1980. But it might have been obvious to someone practicing Open-Air Analysis that $10,000 in Tandy Corporation in the fall of 1978 would be worth $70,000 by the end of 1980. You see, Tandy owns Radio Shack, and those Open-Air customers would have recognized the opportunity when Radio Shack started selling personal computers.

It was also not really obvious in early 1978 that $10,000 invested in a young telecommunications company called Rolm would be worth $80,000 just two years later. But someone practicing Open-Air Analysis might have taken a chance on an over-the-air subscription television company called Oak Industries and, in the same period of time, would have turned $10,000 into $33,000. An Open-Air rookie would spot an Oak Industries; an Open-Air pro would spot Rolm.

An Open-Air rookie, one just starting to practice the art, generally starts his warm-ups by looking at product labels and checking the manufacturer. For instance, anyone living in Los Angeles, Chicago, Miami, Fort Lauderdale, Phoenix, or the Dallas–Fort Worth area should have recognized Oak Industries. This was the corporation serving those cities for over-the-air pay TV. At the end of 1980, they had 450,000 subscribers. There should have been 450,000 very rich people! Because at the beginning of 1979 Oak Industries stock was 17 and it soared to 50 in early 1981. (Throughout this book stock prices will be referred to by numbers only. Dollar signs will be omitted.) All Open-Air practitioners—rookies and pros alike—would have observed the potential in this industry. But the pro would have made the investment.

The rookie sees what's obvious. The pro spots it before it's obvious. Rolm had to be uncovered. We will get to the uncovering process, but first let me introduce the process of Open-Air Analysis and the man who invented the technique. According to him, everyone has the capacity to be an Open-Air analyst. The problem is that most people don't cultivate this unique ability, and those who do rarely learn how to use it with a stockbroker and turn it into profits. That's the purpose of this book.

It all started in 1959 when I first met 100% Schwartz....

The middle booth was for the "big hitters": experienced brokers with high commission income. As a rookie I was put in there to get some experience. Mail and phone, mail and phone—"dialing and smiling," they call it. At any rate, I was floor man the day I met 100% Schwartz. He walked in cold, just a young kid around twenty-four or twenty-five. He made me feel wise and mature at twenty-eight.

Schwartz: What do you think of Brunswick?
Broker: I don't follow it [sounds better than "I don't know"], but I can get you an opinion from research. Do you work for Brunswick?
Schwartz: No. I just bowl a lot and I'm pretty good at it, but, hell, I can't find an alley open anymore, so I thought maybe I'd check into the stock. What's the price?
Broker: 12¾. I can get you a *Standard & Poor*'s sheet or send for an annual report.
Schwartz: Nope, I don't understand all that balance sheet stuff. That's for you guys to figure out—all I know is everyone seems to be bowling. I'll tell

	you, go ahead and get 100 shares, and after you look into it and get that research opinion, if it looks good, give me a call. I may get another 100.
Broker:	Okay, let me open the account. What's your full name?
Schwartz:	John Schwartz.

At lunch we brokers talked about it. A dummy! Do smokers buy cigarette stocks? Do drinkers buy liquor stocks? If you bet on the races, do you buy Hollywood Park? "Just keep dialing for dollars. Don't try to become an analyst; just follow your own firm's recommendations. Make 50 calls a day." I can still hear the New York training routine. The next day I would pass on the firm's opinion. Remember, don't get in the way of an order.

Broker:	Research says it's good for the long term [an opinion often rendered on a "ho-hummer"].
Schwartz:	Okay, buy me another 100 at 12¾.

(Six weeks later, with the stock at $17)

Broker:	You've made a big profit in a short time. You might want to sell half of it, and stick the rest in a box and forget it.
Schwartz:	That's probably a good idea, selling half, but you know something? I'm thinking of buying more because I still can't find an empty bowling alley. In fact, go ahead and buy me another 100 shares.
Broker:	You filled at 17½.

Who is this young guy anyway? When I filled out the new account form, he said he was just hired as a management trainee for Procter & Gamble. He's certainly not sophisticated, or he would not be a walk-in and knowingly do business with a rookie: two rookies trying to make a buck.

When Brunswick reached 25 our firm came out with a recommendation to buy. I called Schwartz with the information. "Guess what stock we just recommended? Brunswick."

Schwartz: I don't have any more money.
Broker: What about margin?
Schwartz: I don't know anything about that margin stuff. Anyway, it might cause me to get nervous and sell it too soon. This stock I'm going to hold for a while.

This was the beginning of my exposure to 100% Schwartz and his Open-Air Analysis. Brunswick climbed through 1959, 1960, and 1961 to almost $75 a share and announced a 2-for-1 split. From an investment of around $4,400, Schwartz had made almost $18,000 in paper profits in three years. The whole world was bowling, and franchising was going crazy. Other bowling stocks like AMF were strong, and it seemed everybody had to have his own bowling alley. 100% Schwartz was a hero that day he came smiling into the office.

Schwartz: How's she doing?
Broker: 68—backed off from that high of 75.
Schwartz: Blow it out!
Broker: You're kidding! It goes ex on the 2-for-1 split in a week, and every brokerage house on Wall Street is recommending it. Why?
Schwartz: Because I can now find empty bowling alleys.

The rest is history. Brunswick fell all the way back to 15 as the oversupply of bowling alleys became well known. Schwartz's Open-Air Analysis worked on the buy side and, most important of all, worked on the sell side. It was obvious when to buy and when to sell only because he was *involved* with his investment, practicing Open-Air, and *bold* enough to put his money where his eyes were.

Every reader can identify with 100% Schwartz. Follow his adventure through this book and experience his baptism by the market. Observe how he becomes a winner by practicing Open-Air Analysis, and in the process you will determine if you have what it takes to be a winner. Watch how he works with a broker and starts a relationship that survives through severe market plunges. As 100% Schwartz observed, "I need a broker who will make me do it. It took years to develop this analysis, but it doesn't work without the right broker who also practices it. When I find that broker, we will both make a fortune."

(2)

USING OPEN-AIR
ANALYSIS TO PICK BOTTOMS

"Lord, get me even and I'll never play this game again."
"I don't want the cheese; just get me out of this trap."

An Open-Air, sure way to tell tops and bottoms is by the number of incoming phone calls to brokerage firms. At tops, brokers can hardly make outgoing calls. Inactive accounts, prospects, and referrals all want on the bandwagon. The whole office is a frenzy: phones are ringing; everyone is on hold; and complaints are piling up. At bottoms, there are no incoming calls. Brokers phone out, and the response is always, "I'll watch it," or "Haven't got any money," or "Just sell the stuff and send me a check."

It was mid-February 1980, and the phones were ringing off the hook. Fifty-million-share days were ho-hummers. The American Stock Exchange and over-the-counter markets were making new all-time highs. Brokers would sell a stock for a client at a good profit, and it would go up another 20%, causing clients to say, "From now on I'm going for the long term and hold everything." Even one broker said, "I'm ordering out my own stocks so I won't sell them." The Dow had pushed up through 900. New margin accounts were being opened, and existing ones were enlarged. (We open margin accounts at tops and close them at bottoms.) "Why am I not in oils?" was the cry. Buzz words like Overthrust, Hibernia,

Beaufort Sea, assets-in-the-ground filled the air. If only IBM had some oil, its stock wouldn't be so weak.

In February 1980, the following verbal question was given to some random clients: where do you want your money right now, and in which order? Their answers:

Real estate
Gold
Silver
Art and collectibles
Oil stocks
Cash

That was the order—get out of all stocks unless they were energy-related. Don't have cash!

It was February 11, and the Dow was just under 920. Some strange things started happening:

Bond prices were in a free fall.
Interest rates were hitting new highs; the prime rate was 15½%.
Gold and silver were soft (but everyone knew it was just a correction).
Real estate had slowed since January.
The new high list was not that big and was primarily made up of natural resource stocks (an ominous sign: remember just before the 1973–74 crash, the last hurrahs were the "nifty fifty" while everything else in the market was weak).

The hostages were still in Iran, and Russia had moved into Afghanistan. Carter and Volcker, in a further attempt to get inflation under control, had tightened the money screws even harder. It was now March 14, 1980, and reserve requirements were raised. Credit card restrictions were imposed, as well as new requirements on the ever-popular money market funds. By March 16, the market had fallen 100 points.

Yields were rising! These moves by Carter and the Fed were thought to be cosmetic—too little too late. But then another fear emerged: what if this drives us into a depression?

The market by now was in full retreat. Interest on margin accounts was 18% and money market funds were paying 14%. An individual on margin said, "Why pay 18% when I could cash out and get 14% on my money?" That's a 32% swing, plus commission, not to mention taxes. Why stay on margin unless you think your stock can go up 40%?

The rout continued: they were giving the market a spring cleaning, and the stock exchanges were having a sale but no one liked the bargains . . . yet. Don Regan, then president of Merrill Lynch (and later secretary of the treasury), had this to say at a luncheon in mid-March: "Institutions are streaming back into equities and out of bonds. They are willing to look over the valley to the new peak. It's only a matter of time until individual investors follow suit. Remember, until this February break, the total return on stock exceeded inflation."

Support is a seven-letter word!

Gold and silver continued to plunge. Auto dealers and home builders were in shock. But there was *one* thing that was going up dramatically—the dollar! The overabundance of dollars in the world was coming home to roost in our high interest rates.

By March 24 the U.S. Treasury notes, 11¾% of 2010, otherwise known as the "Bo Dereks," were selling for 92$^{26}/_{32}$. They had been released at par (100) and, with ever-rising interest rates, had fallen to this point. Interest on margin accounts was now 22%. The prime rate was 20%, and gold had fallen from almost $900 to $500 in two months. The stock market was down 140 points in six weeks, and the American Stock Exchange Index had crashed 30% in thirty trading sessions. Silver plummeted the limit eighteen days in a row, falling from $50 an ounce to $12. A client had purchased one contract on margin for $35,000. He managed to experience only fourteen of the eighteen down days and still lost $70,000: $35,000 was his original investment; he owed the brokerage firm another $35,000.

Then came the bad news! On the morning of March 27, with the market down and then attempting a rally, I noticed a cluster of fellow brokers "huddling up." Any port is a source of refuge in a storm.

"Did you hear the rumor?"

"Which one?"

"Bache sent out a margin call to Nelson Bunker Hunt for $100 million and he can't meet it."

"Great! I'll call my clients who also have had margin calls and tell them they are in good company. Are you serious?"

"Yep. If Bunker Hunt can't meet it, then Bache sells them out."

I went back to my office, and my machine turned into a dive bomber. I'd been through these before: Eisenhower's heart attack; Kennedy's assassination (they suspended trading); May 28 and 29 of 1962 (the tape ran over two hours late); May 1970 (Kent State, hard hats, and high interest); October and December 1974 (high interest rates, Franklin National Bank going under, bank loans up by billions every Thursday); Halloween of 1978 (dollar collapsing, no faith in the president); Halloween of 1979 (Volcker raising interest rates further, 85 million shares traded and market down 25 during midmorning); and now this. . . .

This time it was up to Nelson Bunker Hunt to cause the panic that would establish the bottom, just as it took some form of panic (as above) to establish the previous bottoms. Each time, however, you say to yourself, "Is this the big one?"

It was 2:30 P.M. Eastern time, and the market was down 20. Bache had made its statement about the Hunts and the silver margin call. One broker kept going to the bathroom; another hollered, "I'm getting annihilated!" Another lamented, "We're cleaning out another wave of clients."

All world markets were down. Boeing won the cruise missile over General Dynamics and was down 4. In checking our office margin calls, we found all of them were liquidating stock rather than meeting with cash (a good sign: the market was near its low). We needed despair and panic, and we were getting it. Itel was going to default on its bonds (they were already down to $250 from $1,000 two years ago). The only satisfaction was selling something for a $5,000 loss and feeling smart because afterward it went lower.

Nora New-to-the-Market came running over from her real estate office.

"Get me out, get me out!"
"What if I told you to buy right into this?"
"No way."
"Can I talk you into waiting for this to blow over?"
"Okay."

Another client called and said, "Why is it going down?" Give me a break! "Don't worry, sir, we're just stopping here at this iceberg to take on more ice." This is the type of investor who buys a stock, and when it goes up says, "What's making it go up?"

It was 3:00 P.M., New York time; another broker left for the bar downstairs. A commodity client called, threatening to kill his broker and the office manager. This was reported to the police, and it turned out that he made the same threat to another firm. If there's anything I hate, it's a poor sport. You never know a person until you handle his or her money.

At 3:15 P.M., New York time, the market was at 729,

down 26, but IBM had just turned up ½. "It's turning, it's turning." "Is there any news? This son-of-a-bitch is roaring!" A good sign, just old-fashioned support without any news.

Forty-five minutes later it was over! The market recovered all but five points in the greatest reversal since Serutan. Here's the box score.

> Final-hour volume was 17 million, which was largely *upside* volume.
> There were 714 new lows and 2 highs (Wrigley and a utility preferred).
> Taking out preferreds, there were 476 new lows in the October 1978 decline and 578 this time.
> We closed at 760 on 63,670 million shares.
> Upside volume was 9.6 million and downside volume 52.4 million.
> Largely unnoticed was the fact that yields on T-bills dropped, and the bond market finished up.
> All told, the market fell almost 190 points in seven weeks, which some historians have called a record.
> The American Stock Exchange Index had fallen 30% in only thirty trading sessions.

Below is a random look at how some stocks bounced off their lows in that last forty-five minutes of Bunker Hunt day:

STOCKS	LOW	CLOSE
IBM	51⅜	57¼
Eastman Kodak	44¼	47⅛
Boeing	47¼	54⅜
Inter-City Gas	8⅛	12⅞
Gulf Oil of Canada	95	106¼
GM	44	46
Shearson Loeb Rhoades	19	19⅜
Wainoco Oil	14½	20
Mobil Oil	57	65

As in all panics, it was time to check the stocks that did not make new lows, or better yet, did not go below their 1978 October lows. This is where you might discover the rapid movers in the next upward move. Down markets often tell you much more than up markets.

At lunch we went around the table giving predictions of what the market would do the next day. 90% thought it would be up from 4 to 22 points. It was up 17! One large client placed an order to buy 10,000 Gulf Oil of Canada between 104 and 105 (it had closed at 106¼), but only on the following conditions:

> The market must be down over 10 in the first hour.
> The tape must be ten minutes or more late.

He never got it!

Markets don't bottom overnight. They require backing, filling, and testing. It took three weeks for October 1978 and five weeks for October 1979 (see below). Clients continue to get margin calls, but each test of the old market lows brings fewer and fewer new stock lows.

At bottoms we:

> Get off margin.
> Stop calling in.
> Transfer to another broker.
> Order out stocks.
> Or, as one client put it, "Being in this thing is like following a jack rabbit: you just have to lie low and let the hail storm blow."
> Everyone then starts looking for another "leg down." Why doesn't the public start looking for evidence of the next leg up? Because that's where the money is. Now you know the reason there are very few stock market millionaires.

The Dow Jones Averages
INDUSTRIALS

Courtesy of *The Wall Street Journal*

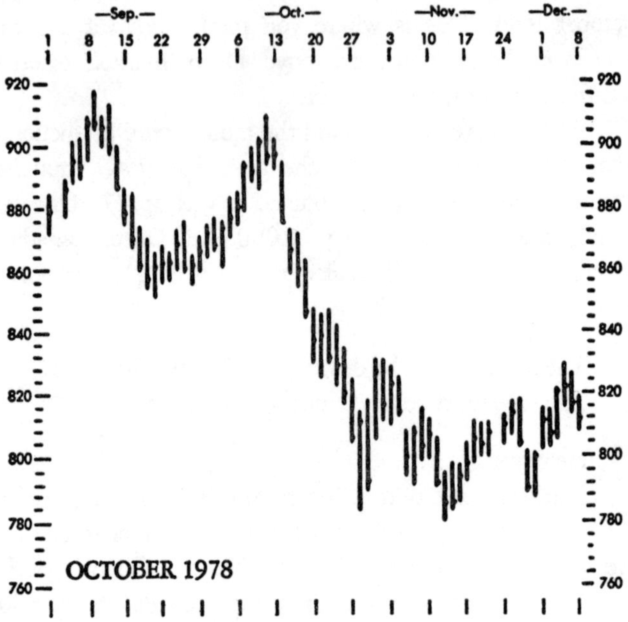

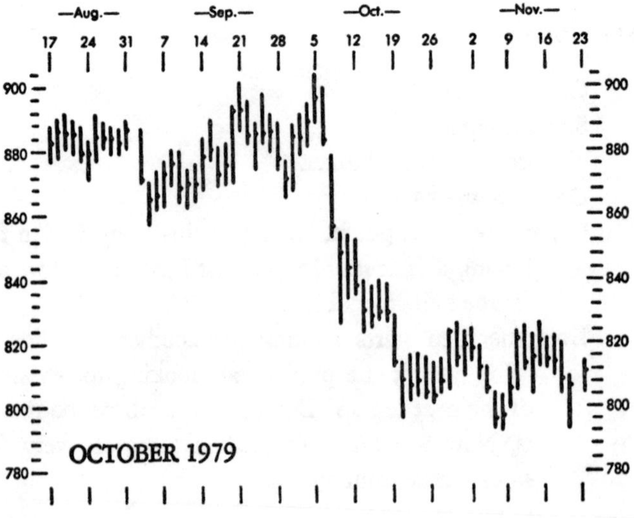

OCTOBER 1978

OCTOBER 1979

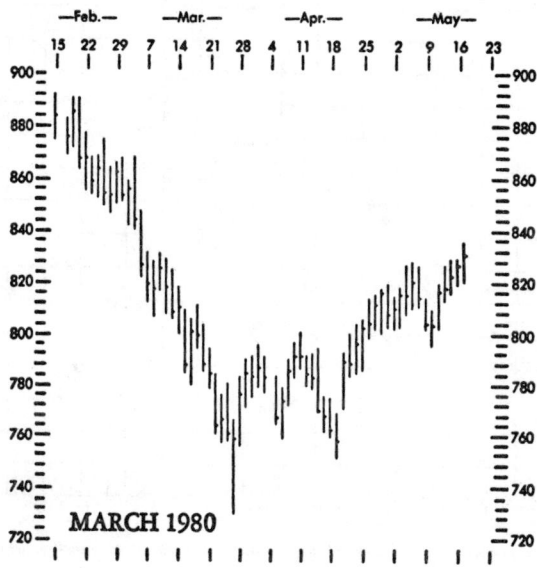

MARCH 1980

The more despair, the more discipline is required to buy. No one buys!

Barring some major international event like war, we were starting the bottoming process. 75% of the phone calls coming in were asking about T-bills and money market funds. By April 5 we had rallied and then fallen back. A look at interest rates during this period shows what was happening.

Sufficient fear can be a self-correcting mechanism. When there is tremendous demand for T-bills, the government doesn't have to pay as much interest to attract buyers. Interest rates can start down in this climate.

Visualize interest rates to look like a snake. The head of the snake is Fed funds and T-bills; the middle part of the snake is the prime rate; and the tail is mortgage rates. The head can be going around a corner and going down while the body and tail are still going up. The prime is meaningless: it merely adjusts to the Fed fund rate and T-bill rate.

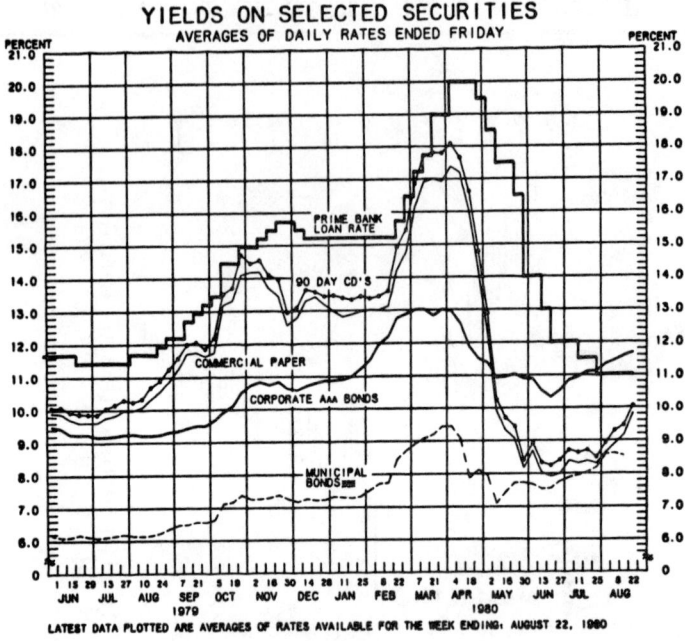
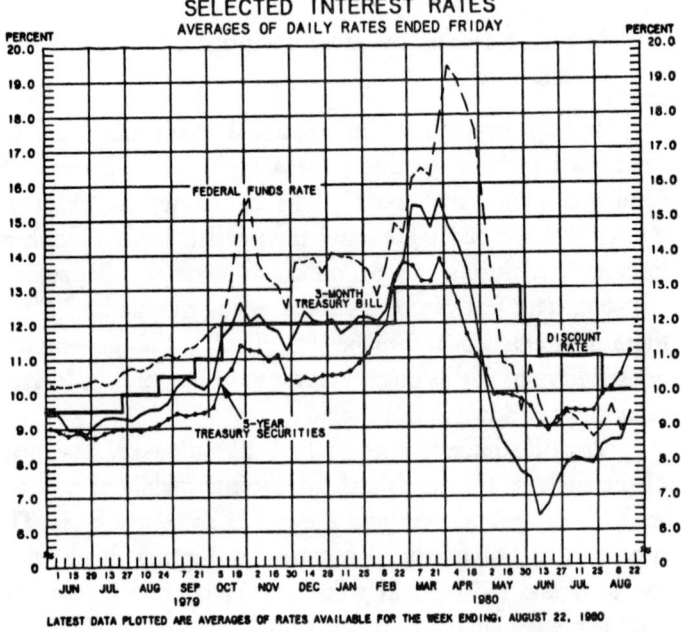

Prepared by Federal Reserve Bank of St. Louis

USING OPEN-AIR ANALYSIS TO PICK BOTTOMS

"Interest rates are peaking?"

We were then rallying and dive-bombing. Whatever it took to move stocks from weak hands to strong was occurring, but all the time interest rates kept coming down. The difference in making money and getting rich is often dictated by timing. Was that the time? *Yes!* But the phone calls at bottoms are almost always initiated by the brokers, and most are greeted with, "Only an idiot would buy stocks now."

SOME MONEY MARKET WAR STORIES

On April Fool's Day, 1980, the municipal bond buyer index was 9.44%. On April 23, it was 7.89%. That translates into a 16% *increase* in the price of the tax-exempt bond index. This is the equivalent of 130 points up on the Dow. Twenty-three days for a 16% gain in muni-bonds—wow! Nothing excites Wall Street like declining interest rates. It's as if Paul

Revere came riding through the stock exchange yelling "Interest rates are peaking, interest rates are peaking!"

Those "Bo Dereks" 11¾% of 2010 that were selling at 92^{26}/$_{32}$ on March 24 hit 107 bid on April 16. Anyone buying these on margin and putting up 10% doubled his money in about three weeks. Yes, in a U.S. government bond!

On April 18, the money supply dropped dramatically: M1-A and M1-B were down $2½ billion. On April 22, the Dow had dropped back down slightly below the 760 recovery high of Bunker Hunt day. A client sold her Ford stock ⅛ above a 22-year low, "because they were going under." This was Nora New-to-the-Market. I talked her out of it once, but not this time. That afternoon, T-bills (at the Monday auction) dropped almost 200 basis points, and the market rallied 30 points the next day. T-bills had now dropped from 16½ to 12%.

In the week of April 25, the money supply was down another $2½ billion.

Joe Granville, an investment advisor with a big following, put out a buy signal, and that contributed to the 30-point upswing. Using some Open-Air Analysis comparisons, remember that test that was given back in mid-February? The one where cash finished last? Well, I gave it again, and the results were: "We're going into a depression." "The only thing I want now is cash." In a little over two months, cash had moved from the bottom of the list to the top. At some future point, with the Dow screaming up 200 points and my incoming calls swamping me, someone will say, "Why didn't you get me into this before it moved?"

Three agonizing months, including six weeks of straight decline, and six weeks of aftershock. Alan Abelson of *Barron's* summed it up well: "Can we just cancel the rest of 1980? The bond market really ended up in the Smithsonian. The stock market fell down an air shaft. The prime rate hit 20% and inflation maintained a nice steady 18–19%. A fat Texan with a passion for corners and completely bereft of the wit to negotiate them, brought down the silver market, made Wall Street's teeth rattle, and threatened the worst financial panic since Jay Gould tried to corner gold."

Then on April 25, another bombshell of an announcement: our rescue mission for the hostages in Iran had failed. The Dow was up 6! Much like Kennedy in the Bay of Pigs or Eisenhower with the U-2, the net result of an international embarrassment had little effect on Wall Street. Maybe we weren't so weak after all. Speaking of weakness, why wasn't the market down on this news? Had the bottom been seen? The London market had now fallen to 435 from over 500. Gold was down to 513. The First Pennsylvania Bank, the nation's 23rd largest, was saved from going under by the FDIC and other banks with a $500 million bailout. Mortgage rates had fallen to 12%, and Paine Webber's continuing management training program switched from the Waldorf to the basement of the Holiday Inn in Norwalk, Connecticut.

The bottom *was* made, and the market was starting up. The Hunt brothers were not so fortunate. Who would have thought Nelson Bunker Hunt could not meet a margin call? But on Bunkie Hunt day, March 27, 1980, the brothers reportedly lost $1 billion, at least on paper. They had owned some 200 million ounces of silver, bought since 1974 at prices ranging from $4 to $30 an ounce. They cornered one-sixth of the free world's entire stock of silver. In January 1980, their holdings were worth $10 billion. By March 26, they had dwindled to $3.2 billion. Bache Halsey Stuart Shields issued a margin call for $100 million, and when the Hunts could not meet it, they started unloading collateral: securities, bullion, and, of course, silver. The brothers Hunt would not file for unemployment, however. Tiffany & Co. took out the following ad in *The New York Times* two days after Bunker Hunt day:

> **UNCONSCIONABLE**
>
> We think it is unconscionable for anyone to hoard several billion, yes billion, dollars worth of silver and thus drive the price up so high that others must pay artificially high prices for articles made of silver, from baby spoons to tea sets, as well as photographic film and other products.
>
> **TIFFANY & CO.**
> NEW YORK

Courtesy of Tiffany & Co.

Open-Air Analysis does not concern itself just with converting an observation into a single stock selection. It senses public moods, changes in fashion, shifts in buying habits, and bottoms in stock markets. *It's the secret of success!*

Broker: Well, Schwartz, we're taking gas. March 1980 is going into the record books.
Schwartz: I hope not alongside October 1929. It's cratering. What are you going to do?
Broker: Ride it out. What's your Open-Air say?
Schwartz: This one might be worse than October '78 and

'79, because we've got to come down from 20% interest rates. But let's get out our basket.

Broker: The best thing that can happen to the market is a one-year recession. Remember '75 and '76? We had great stock and bond markets while inflation was winding down to 4.8% when Carter took over.

Schwartz: I went to Ruff's seminar last night.

Broker: I heard he had five thousand people.

Schwartz: Yeah, I remember that at the end of the sixties they would put on a seminar about how to get rich in the stock market, and hundreds would show up. Right next door would be a seminar on buying real estate, and there would be ten to fifteen people.

Broker: What's your point?

Schwartz: When it comes to investment seminars, always buy what's in least attendance. No one but an Open-Air member might have suspected the beginning of a change then—a slow ending to the attraction of stocks and the beginning of real estate.

Broker: And?

Schwartz: Well, right next to Howard Ruff's seminar about bad times was a room where some broker was talking about "Is This the Time to Be Buying Stocks?"

Broker: How many were there?

Schwartz: Four. Me and three others—and they were teenagers.

Broker: Did you tell them I'm a broker for the future?

Schwartz: Open-Air tries to see the future today, and it often means be a contrarian. Everyone was lining up to hear about stocks at the end of their ten-year move in the sixties. Now they are lining up to buy condos and gold and silver in the fall of 1979, and Open-Air says watch out! Incidentally, let's average down on Ford. I bought the first 500 at what?

Broker: 27¾.

Schwartz: It made a twenty-two-year low yesterday and goes ex-dividend in three days. Okay, buy me another 500 at market. Last trade was 24, right? If my Open-Air says, "Buy whatever you have to wait in line for," then let's pick up some oils for our basket. What's your firm like in oils?

Broker: Wait a minute—you're inconsistent! You just get through saying to buy what's in least attendance. Now you're saying buy what you have to wait in line for.

Schwartz: Dammit, I thought you were already baptized on Open-Air. It often picks bottoms and changes in investment philosophy by detecting what is out of favor. The opposite happens when Open-Air starts picking individual stocks—that's when it looks for the crowd to start forming, or waiting in line. Now, what about those oils?

Broker: Standard of Indiana, Mobil, and Exxon. The firm also likes some younger exploratory companies like Juniper and Wainoco.

Schwartz: Well, it's just obvious; it's obvious.

Broker: What's obvious?

Schwartz: It took the people of this country six years to even believe there was an energy crisis. They thought it was the oil companies causing all the problems.

Broker: Having obscene profits?

Schwartz: It's obvious that you buy whatever you're running out of and also buy the companies that have to drill for it.

Broker: Like Hughes Tool, Halliburton, Schlumberger,

and Santa Fe International. Your Open-Air is cooking.

Schwartz: Which ones would you buy?

Broker: Stay with U.S. oil and don't fool around with companies that have stakes in foreign companies.

Schwartz: Such as . . . ?

Broker: Standard of Indiana, Standard of Ohio; and Juniper is big in the Overthrust.

Schwartz: Okay. Let's put $10,000 in each. What are the prices?

Broker: Juniper is $15\frac{1}{2}$ down from $21\frac{1}{4}$; Standard of Indiana is 100; and Standard of Ohio is 91.

Schwartz: Go ahead and get 100 each of Indiana and Ohio and 600 Juniper. When I'm sitting in the gas lines, at least I won't feel so bad every time they raise the price.

Broker: Yes, but you wouldn't buy housing stocks on that basis. With rising home prices, there's a point of no return in the cost of money, plus the cost of housing. They finally price themselves out of the market.

Schwartz: You need oil and you don't need to own a house. What are some speculations that look good now?

Broker: Are you sure you want to speculate in this environment?

Schwartz: Open-Air says you become a speculator at bottoms and an investor at tops. Most people do the opposite.

Broker: Tell me about it; after a big decline, they say, "Get me out of Tom Brown, Commodore International, Tandy, Computervision, and into money markets."

Schwartz: Open-Air says to buy oil, energy, synfuel, and anything connected with improving productivity. That's the buzz word.

Broker: Okay. We got another good Open-Air sign today, 100%. The University of Michigan survey said consumer confidence was at a thirty-four-year low.

Schwartz: That's what that fellow said last night in that seminar—the only way you're going to get someone else's stock away from him cheaply is by taking advantage of his pessimism and fear.

Broker: Did you know that's how J. Paul Getty and Howard Hughes increased their big stakes? They bought the hell out of stocks in the depression.

Schwartz: Everyone forgets that they started their fortunes in the depression, buying all that cheap stock. Incidentally, I went shopping on one of my Open-Air field trips.

Broker: Looking for stocks instead of merchandise.

Schwartz: Right, and I think I found three. Are you ready for this? It's April 1980, and two observations have filtered through my Open-Air net: we are in a country-and-western craze, and stores have found a slick way to fight pilferage.

Broker: Okay, what's the story this time?

Schwartz: I went shopping in my mall asking the usual questions about what's hot and what's new and found out the whole world is buying cowboy hats and boots. Furthermore, there is a new device, a tag, that fits on articles and gives off a warning by means of microwaves. The electronic article surveillance industry is going to be built around this contraption.

Broker: You mean Sensormatic and Knogo; but what's obvious? I mean, what do you buy to participate in the western craze?

Schwartz: Tony Lama boots. What are the prices?

Broker:	Knogo is 27¼; Sensormatic is 26; and Tony Lama boots is 7.
Schwartz:	Well, Tony Lama is probably a short-term deal, but the other two look like the beginning of a new industry. Crime goes for 30 times earnings. What are their P/Es?
Broker:	Sensormatic is 12 times; Knogo is 10 times; and Tony Lama boots is 5 times. You want their dividends?
Schwartz:	Hey, you know me better than that. When I start asking about dividends, I'm either bearish or operating with scared money. Buy me 500 Knogo and 200 Sensormatic and 500 Tony Lama. Then let's check them out and think about buying more.
Broker:	I'm surprised you're not buying Eastman Kodak, with the price of silver collapsing. If ever there was an Open-Air evaluation, that's it!
Schwartz:	By God, I knew you'd earn your keep some day. What's the price?
Broker:	Fifty bucks! This stock used to be 150 and was in the high 60s before all this hit the fan. It's a 6% yield and sells for 8 times earnings down here.
Schwartz:	I don't need anymore. Buy me 500. Let's get the basket out! We may have to sit with these cheap stocks for several months, but when she starts up, we're on the train with a seat next to the window.
Broker:	And as usual, when the train starts out of the station, everyone is looking, but not getting on.
Schwartz:	Until we've gone quite a way.

⦅3⦆

HOW TO MAKE MONEY THROUGH THE USE OF OPEN-AIR ANALYSIS

―――――•―――――

The obvious can be rewarding until everyone knows it, then what everyone knows isn't worth knowing.

Isn't it all speculation? Yes. But the word *speculate* needs proper clarification. The word has sinister connotations, yet Columbus and Alexander Graham Bell were speculators. So were John D. Rockefeller, Henry Ford, Edwin Land of Polaroid, and Jonas Salk. *Speculation* can be abused, but the true definition comes from the Latin word *speculare*, which means to perceive. The old Roman "speculation" was a tower where one (a speculator) could observe and foresee unfolding developments and act upon them *before* other people who were less farsighted and without the benefit of a tower. Today Open-Air Analysis is our tower. If we are able to develop it and accurately perceive the changes taking place in our society, the stock market opportunities are unlimited.

How does it work? Generally, it starts to operate when it perceives three things: a trend, a breakthrough, or a problem. The first two are obvious, but how do you make money by recognizing problems? It is in finding the solutions to those problems that profits are created.

For example, in 1978, a close examination of the demography of this country revealed a population explosion of senior citizens coming on the scene in the eighties. Did those of you who found waiting lists for nursing homes in the last few years consider nursing home and health care stocks? As Schwartz says, "I always buy what I have to wait in line for," especially if it has not been reflected in the market, and at many nursing homes there was a waiting list. The problem was a shortage of beds, and the solution to the shortage was greater access to health care and nursing facilities. Another new industry had been formed out of the big umbrella called health care. It was called hospital management: taking over inefficient hospitals or nursing homes. If these Open-Air stocks had been purchased on June 30, 1978, and held through the three bad breaks of October 1978, October 1979, and March 1980, they would have appreciated as follows:

	PRICE 6/30/78	PRICE 8/30/80
American Medical International	19⅞	48¼
Beverly Enterprises	5⅝	17⅞
Hospital Corp. of America	15¾	45¾
Humana	10½	53¼
Lifemark	9⅞	31
National Medical Enterprises	13	43½

Another example of recognizing a problem and then "buying" the solution was in oil. The solution was in finding more oil or energy. Who specializes in finding oil? An Open-Air, logical approach is to look at the oil service companies—the drillers:

	PRICE 6/30/78	PRICE 8/30/80
Hughes Tool	24	68½
Reading & Bates	15½	53⅝
Schlumberger	54	133
Santa Fe International	29	53
Zapata	15¼	53½

Is solar energy the new industry of the eighties? Will there be fortunes made as a result of the creation of the synfuel industry? All these are solutions to problems that will be discussed in the last chapter.

What about spotting a breakthrough? It doesn't have to be a new technological product like computer aid design (Computervision); it might be a breakthrough in legislation ... like New Jersey's approving gambling in 1977.

	PRICE 6/30/78	PRICE 6/30/79
Bally Manufacturing	19	42
Caesars World	5¼	28
Resorts International-A	24	41

All of us who have ever visited Las Vegas or Reno could have made back our losses tenfold had we stepped back in the open air and thought about the future of gambling once it was legalized.

It's tough to acquire the vision that must go hand in hand with Open-Air Analysis, especially when it's right in front of you. Take the true story of thirty stockbrokers, all members of a prominent West Coast bond club. In the spring of 1977 they held their annual bond club outing as guests of Caesars Palace. In fact, the controller of Caesars was the brother of one of the brokers. They golfed, partied, and were treated to a free dinner, compliments of the management. Management even gave a short presentation on the future of gambling and Caesars. The stock was $4. Only two brokers came back and bought it, but sold it out at 12 for a short-term trade. Caesars rose to 36 in the next two years. It had two splits: a 3 for 2 and a 3 for 1.

The moral of the story? Open-Air is often right under our noses. As one broker remarked to his clients in the early sixties, "You don't need me, just go to a McDonald's or a Kentucky Fried Chicken and try to get waited on."

Does the legislation breakthrough about deregulation of airlines, railroads, and communications offer the same opportunities? We will discuss this and similar opportunities in the chapter entitled "Profits in the Eighties."

So you pick out some winners and try to make a case for the *entire* stock market. What about the losers? What has the stock market ever done for you? You will not only find out about the losers in this book, you will also discover what type of investor seems to get more losers than winners. For now, let's concentrate on how we use Open-Air to be a winner.

Have you ever had the really big winner—the one you held all the way and, in fact, bought more of whenever it dropped? That one good investment? Let's see what Open-Air Analysis might have uncovered in the past. When client and broker use it together, it is a winner.

For example: with the arrival of the miniskirts in 1967, women were also introduced to panty hose. From 1966 to 1968 panty hose went from 20% to 80% of total women's hosiery. How many women bought their first pair, thought it was a terrific deal, but did not analyze what was taking place? By just standing back in the open air and observing, they might have gone to their brokers and bought Hanes, the manufacturer of L'eggs. $10,000 invested in Hanes toward the end of 1967 would have been worth $20,000 one year later. Hanes is now a subsidiary of Consolidated Foods.

Or in 1971, how many people who purchased their first set of contact lenses were able to convert that experience into profits in Bausch & Lomb? $10,000 in June 1970 in Bausch & Lomb had grown to over $20,000 by June 1973. Again, when the soft contact lenses were introduced, $10,000 in Bausch & Lomb climbed to over $30,000 from early 1979 to the end of 1980: a chance to get rich twice on the same stock.

Or in 1973, when Rival Manufacturing pioneered the Crock-Pot; if you and your broker had used simple Open-Air logic, you might have thought, "Can you believe what this thing will do for working wives?" Ten grand in Rival late that year (a bad year in the stock market) was still worth $50,000 by early 1976.

Or in 1975, coming out of the recession, how many observed the pent-up demand for housing that was later to cause real estate to go crazy? If you and your broker were using Open-Air Analysis, you might have participated by owning Coldwell Banker stock. $10,000 in late 1975 was worth $50,000 by the fall of 1978! You didn't need to buy real estate itself, just the stock market equivalent.

Or in 1977, if you were an ulcer patient and had been given Tagamet by your doctor, did it occur to you to ask your broker about SmithKline Corporation? It tripled in just over a year!

Or in 1977, how many people who saw *Star Wars* used that experience to double their money in Twentieth Century-Fox stock in a year?

Or those of you who work in offices: when word processors started to become popular in 1976 and 1977, an Open-Air discussion with your broker might have resulted in the purchase of Wang Laboratories stock. $10,000 in the fourth quarter of 1977 was worth $70,000 by the third quarter of 1980.

We have discussed what should have happened to your money-making senses while you were waiting in those gas lines. One enterprising stockbroker even hired a kid to hand out his firm's recommendations on oil stocks. The kid was instructed to walk up and down the lines and hand them to everyone driving a Lincoln, Cadillac, Mercedes, or Porsche. No response! The broker tried to "make them do it," but no one was aware of Open-Air Analysis.

But not every movie means a stock fortune, and some trends are merely fads that cause temporary excitement and then collapse. Just ask the investors who didn't get out of the calculator, double knit, or CB radio crazes soon enough. A drug can seem like the greatest advance in science, but remember what the Thalidomide event did to Richardson Merrill stock? Not every technology breakthrough is a winner; just ask the investor who bought Itel in January of 1978 at 14 and rode it up to 36 in August, then saw it at 12 by June 1979 and down to 2 by August 1980. On a scale of ten, Itel was a ten: computer leasing and the first company to seriously challenge IBM . . . until certain red flags started waving. How do you spot those red flags, and who brings them to your attention? That chapter is close at hand.

How can a layman develop Open-Air Analysis? Does it require that he be in business or have a college degree? Most definitely not, but it does require reading and many, many field trips. Open-Air is achieved by crossing observation with common sense mixed with a high degree of curiosity. What can you read? *Barron's, The Wall Street Journal, Business Week, Fortune,* and *Forbes* are a must, and they are tax deductible. Supplement your daily newspaper with *The New York Times* (get it at the library or subscribe to the Sunday home delivery), trade journals like *The Oil and Gas Journal, Computer World,* or *Electronic News,* and then, most important of all, instruct your broker to inundate you with research material. Remember, Wall Street often runs in herds and it is well to know what the herd is thinking, even if you do go in the opposite direction. How else will you know what is opposite?

Next, when you are at the restaurant, ask the manager, "What's new in restaurants?" At the gas station, ask, "What's new in equipment?" or, "How's the allotment?" At the supermarket, "What's new in the food business?" At the movies, "What is the next biggie?" On the airplane, "How's traffic?" At the doctor, "Any new wonder drugs?" At the car dealer, "How are sales, and what is the big seller?" At the department store, "How's business?" or just be mindful of the parking lot. You can find winners at conventions. Go to the medical, electronic, and computer conventions. For example, if you had gone to the toy convention in July 1980 and seen Mattel's Intellivision you might have bought the stock. It went from 8 to 15 right after the convention. Be a nosey pest. The other person is always flattered anyway. And watch the kids—the greatest trend-setters of all. Just ask the parent who has bought Levi's for the last five years—but probably never thought of owning the stock.

But beware—not every new cereal makes a big impact on General Foods. Barbie Doll once made Mattel stock more than triple, but it takes a big, big winner to have a significant earnings increase on a company with a $500 million sales base or larger. Everyone thought Greyhound stock would go to the moon after the Arab oil embargo, but close examination revealed a very volatile division within Greyhound called Armour. They can have a great year with bus revenues only to be washed out by losses in their meat operations.

This is where a good broker comes in. Many losses occurred in the seventies as a result of false starts in coal stocks. There was a glut of coal, and environmental restrictions were killing it, but Open-Air Analysis might have caused you to buy coal unless you first checked it out with your broker.

If Open-Air is to be used in buying, it is even *more* important in selling. Anyone can buy stocks, but not everyone can sell them. Even the biggest nuclear accident in our history at Three Mile Island could not dislodge some investors from the parent company General Public Utilities. The sell decision can be either the guillotine or slow torture. It can be Equity Funding, which one had only about one day to sell before the stock was suspended for several years, or it can be slow declines over two years like Caesars World falling from a high of 36 in 1979 to a low of 10 in 1980.

Believe it or not, it is harder for most people to sell a

stock that has gone from 20 to 50 than it is to sell a stock that has done nothing for two years. It is therefore more difficult to utilize Open-Air on the sell side, because the investor has been lulled into taking good performance for granted. To be a good seller, you must become increasingly critical the higher your stocks climb. This does not mean to have a selling frame of mind just because a stock moves up 20% in a few months, but once you own a doubler, get closer to the field of play. When a baseball manager is way ahead because his portfolio of nine players has been performing well, he doesn't risk losing the game when *one* player, his pitcher, starts to crack. He brings in a substitute.

As recently as 1978, the phenomenon of working wives, coupled with the big move to jeans and ready-to-wear, presented ominous evidence for a company like Singer. Open-Air logic said get out, and Singer slowly sank from its high of 24 in 1978 to a low of 6¼ in 1980. The same slow torture affected the Avon stockholder: there were no working wives at home to answer "Avon calling." In 1973 Avon was 138; at the bottom of the bad 1974 market, it was 18. That's not torture, that's gas! By 1980 it still had only recovered to 35. Millionaires were made in Avon in the fifties and sixties. It caused margin calls in the seventies. Fame is fleeting!

Don't worry about getting a divorce from a stock that hasn't treated you well—it doesn't know you own it. Let's examine a list of stocks and how they performed from June 30, 1978, to June 30, 1980, after adjustments for all splits and stock dividends.

	JU 1
American Airlines (airlines)	1
Cessna Aircraft (private aircraft)	
Church's Fried Chicken (fast foods)	

	JUNE 1978	JUNE 1980
Collins Foods (fast foods)	15⅞	10½
Dayco (rubber, v-belts, etc.)	14¾	10⅝
Delta Airlines (airlines)	45½	40
Envirotech (pollution control, mining machinery)	24	9¾
Firestone (tires)	14	6⅞
Ford (automobiles)	46¾	24¾
Fotomat (photography stores)	14⅝	5⅛
General Motors (automobiles)	59½	47
General Public Utilities (Three Mile Island)	18½	5⅞
Goodyear (tires)	16⅞	13
Itek (optics, graphics)	31½	18
Itel (computer leasing)	23⅜	3¼
K mart (discount merchandising)	24½	22½
Massey Ferguson (farm machinery, engines)	10½	6¾
Memorex (computer equipment, magnetic media)	46	14⅝
Outboard Marine (outboard motors)	21½	9⅞
Sambo's Restaurants (restaurants)	18¾	4¼
Sears (retail sales)	23⅛	17
Sheller-Globe (automotive parts)	12	5¾
Stauffer Chemical (industrial chemicals, plastics)	40⅛	17⅝
Triangle Pacific (home cabinets, floors)	20⅛	18⅛
Tyler Corporation (pipes, fittings)	27	11¼
U. S. Steel (largest steel maker)	26½	18⅞
Webb Corporation, Del (gambling)	21½	11⅜
Western Airlines (airlines)	11	7⅛
White Motor Company (trucks, farm equipment)	10⅛	3⅞

An Open-Air evaluation during this period suggests the following: you can overbuild casinos just like bowling alleys, calculators, panty hose, or Crock-Pots. Also take a look at the fast-food chains. How many of us as fast-food stockholders started witnessing Denny's, Sambo's, McDonald's, and Taco Bells appearing on every corner. The tire stocks were a different story—they should have won the Nobel Prize for corporate integrity because they produced a product that lasted *too long*; it almost sank Firestone. Pure Open-Air could observe that as the price of oil increased, it would seriously affect things like autos and airlines that consume oil. And it doesn't take the president of the New York Stock Exchange to see that steel stocks would be affected by cars getting smaller and lighter. When your stocks are going down, the first-stage reaction is, "This is a correction." The second stage is, "I think it will come back" (meaning "I hope"). And finally, "Just get me out." Open-Air can at least keep you from the second and third stages.

Have you made money in the stock market in the last several years? You should have.

In addition to those stocks already mentioned, let's look at an extensive list of stocks that performed *well* during that same period from June 30, 1978, to June and August 1980. (We are constantly using this period because it challenges three very sharp corrections in the market. Otherwise, you can pick any period you want to justify almost any theory in stock market investing.)

But let's examine this list, admittedly from a hindsight viewpoint, but with the hope that the same thinking process can be used for future profits. Which of these stocks could have been uncovered by using Open-Air Analysis? By August 30, 1980, $10,000 invested in June 1978 would have been approximately worth the figure in parenthesis:

Alpha Industries ($46,000)—microwave devices
American Brands ($16,000)—tobacco, food, insurance

ASA ($25,900)—South African gold, closed end
Benguet ($40,000)—gold in the Philippines
Campbell Red Lake ($36,875)—Canadian gold mining
Cenvill Communities ($21,700)—adult residential communities
Chieftain Development ($38,100)—oil and gas drilling
Chris-Craft ($20,000)—boats, TV stations
Christiana Companies ($20,000)—real estate development
Cincinnati Milacron ($28,000)—robots for industry, machine tools
City Investing ($17,375)—housing, insurance, financial
Coastal States Gas ($18,800)—oil
Commodore International ($52,300)—consumer electronics, home computers
Delhi International Oil ($115,000)—oil
Dome Mines ($43,000)—Canadian gold
Dome Petroleum ($48,600)—Canadian oil
Engelhard Mineral ($42,725)—minerals, ores, precious metals
Esterline ($37,222)—analytical instrumentation
First Mississippi ($32,800)—chemicals, fertilizers
Flight Safety International ($33,200)—aircraft and marine training
Fluor ($36,100)—oil and gas refinery construction
GCA ($51,250)—semiconductor products
Geosource ($33,075)—oil drilling
Gerber Scientific ($40,500)—computer-automated drafting systems
Global Marine ($76,600)—oil drilling
G K Technology ($22,775)—fiber optics, cables
Helmerich & Payne ($34,275)—contract oil driller
Hutton, E. F. ($24,500)—stock brokerage
Magma Power ($28,000)—geothermal energy
Mitchell Energy ($42,200)—oil, gas, real estate

N L Industries ($28,100)—petroleum services
Nucor ($29,700)—mini steel mills
Paradyne ($43,300)—data communications equipment
Petro Lewis ($30,000)—oil and gas
Pioneer Corporation ($34,200)—oil and gas
Rolm ($51,400)—telecommunications
Sedco ($24,100)—offshore drilling
Shearson Loeb Rhoades ($48,300)—stock brokerage
Staley, A. E. ($24,000)—corn, soybean products
Standard of California ($18,250)—major oil company
Standard of Indiana ($24,166)—major oil company
Technicolor ($30,000)—color film processor
Texas Oil and Gas ($43,300)—oil and gas
Tidewater ($23,177)—supplies to offshore rigs
U. S. Home ($31,400)—leading homebuilder
Viacom International ($22,400)—cable TV
Wainoco ($43,500)—oil exploration
Wang Laboratories ($48,000)—word processors
Waste Management ($30,600)—solid chemical waste management services

A moment's diversion for the benefit of those obsessed with ratings: how many of the above were rated A or better? Seven. For performance, it's the old story of buy them when they're nonrated; hold them when they're B-rated; and sell them when they're A-rated.

Open-Air hindsight? Looking back, it's easy to see that you simply bought stocks during that period in companies whose products and services were in big demand—oil, oil drilling, minerals, and home building. People were in a home-buying frenzy (get it quick before the price goes up). Companies like Commodore International, Computervision, Wang, and Gerber Scientific were beginning to make their presence felt in high-technology areas such as personal computers, computer-aided drafting equipment for architects and draftsmen, and word processors. $10,000 invested in these four companies at their 1979 low prices was worth the following by October 17, 1980:

Commodore International	$151,428
Computervision	106,666
Gerber Scientific	58,750
Wang Laboratories	41,785

If you gain nothing else out of this book, gain this: what seems so necessary today may not even be desirable tomorrow. The difference between making money and getting rich in the stock market is the *ability to be ahead of your time*. The obvious was apparent in oils and technology even late in the game. You bought after something had already doubled, and it still went up another 50%. But the big, big winners are Open-Air Analyzers who are willing to be early. There is only one penalty for being ahead of your time: it's called "having to wait." Most of us can't wait.

From September 15, 1976, to September 15, 1977, the stock of Rolm, a telecommunications company, traded between 1¼ and 1⅞ on an adjusted basis. In the next three years ending September 15, 1980, it rose to 40. Depending on where you started, 1¼ or 1⅞, $10,000 went to $213,353 or $320,000. Tommy Today might have grown impatient and said, "Let's get into something that's moving." But Terry Tomorrow kept studying their progress, and she concluded, "They're continuing to do well; they're in a great area; and telecommunications is a big growth industry. Even *Business Week* called it the fastest growth area of the eighties." As we will come to appreciate in later chapters, Terry's main obstacle was not impatience but managing her position, especially when the stock went from 1½ to 5 or 6. It is so easy to justify selling on the basis of "you can't go wrong taking a profit." Selling at 5 or 6 on the way to 40 is typical, especially after waiting a year.

Always get out when there is a sales drop in a quarterly earnings report. The exception to this might be where sales are down because of discontinued operations. But be out if there are consecutive drops in earnings. However, by then, it might be too late. Open-Air tries to alert you to the environment that could cause an earning or sales drop *before* it happens, even if it doesn't occur for a year. Take the classic case of Sears. An *A+ rating* on this stock was small comfort while it sank from 50 in early 1973 to 15 in 1980. The bowling alley observation was appropriate here. The rapid rise of the discounts and the mail-order catalog stores like Walmart and Best provided the Sears customer with the ability to say, "I don't have to go to Sears anymore to get a discount."

Could the same thing be happening to big, A+ rated American Telephone? Let's compare some *nonrated* telecommunication companies with American Telephone:

	1978 LOW	NOVEMBER 1980
American Telephone	56⅞	47⅝
MCI Communications	3¼	14¼
Graphic Scanning	12	34
Rolm	1½	44
TIE Communications (came public in 1979 at 2¾)		15
Southern Pacific (communications)	25	45

It's heresy for a stockbroker to recommend selling A+ rated stocks, especially when all the bank trust officers are buying them. So if you and your broker can't make a selling decision, then let Open-Air Analysis do it.

In summary, Open-Air Analysis starts in the field and ends in the brokerage office. Most of us work in the other direction. The observation or experience should be brought to the attention of the broker where the analysis begins. The hot drug stock is being bought by the doctors or pharmacists, and the engineers are buying the new electronic breakthrough. Wall Street, by nature, picks on something that has *already* started moving. But if you're out among them doing your field trips and practicing Open-Air, you might get on that big winner early.

Broker: Well, the rescue attempt for the hostages failed. The helicopters broke down.

Schwartz: Who makes helicopters?

Broker: United Technology for one. But forget it; we've got another problem. The heat and drought in Texas have already killed over a hundred people and damaged crops severely. We could get a big rise in food prices this winter.

Schwartz: Who makes air conditioners? And let's buy a fertilizer stock like First Mississippi.

Broker: Aren't you carrying Open-Air a little too far? If I told you a flu epidemic broke out in New Orleans and killed fifty people you'd . . .

Schwartz: . . . want to buy a drug stock that makes flu vaccine. Actually I'm serious now. I attend every seminar or lecture that's not too expensive. It's part of my Open-Air field work, and, of course, it's paid off.

Broker: What's the latest?

Schwartz: Last night the speaker said that in five years none of us will have to drive our cars to hear him speak. It will all be done with breakthroughs in telecommunications. Get me a rundown on that industry.

Broker: Some very interesting stocks like MA/COM, MCI Communications, TIE Communications. I've been buying the MCI because they've grown

	to be second only to AT&T in long-distance telephone revenues used by businesses. We have a write-up on MCI that I'll show you.
Schwartz:	They have that lawsuit pending against the telephone company, don't they?
Broker:	Yes, but they are now branching into residential use—all with microwave. Which brings up MA/COM.
Schwartz:	Wait . . . I'm taking notes. What's MCI and what are the earnings?
Broker:	5½. Earnings could be 40–45¢ in 1980 and double in 1981 and 1982. They are underselling Ma Bell by 30% and taking on residential customers at an enormous clip.
Schwartz:	And MA/COM?
Broker:	23.
Schwartz:	Tell me about MA/COM.
Broker:	The old Microwave Associates; they're a leading supplier of equipment for commercial and governmental satellite communication. They serve the telecommunications and data communications markets. They are also in the fiber-optics business, which is the breakthrough for transmitting sound or light. They have also developed a technique for transmitting television over fiber-optic cables.
Schwartz:	You have all the buzz words.
Broker:	This whole telecommunications industry reminds me of the electronic industry in the early sixties. And MA/COM is like the Texas Instruments of that era. No matter which direction the industry takes, it needs microwave components, and MA/COM is the one.
Schwartz:	P/E of 12 but growing 25%. Have you called the company?

Broker: Not yet.
Schwartz: Call me after you find out. In the meantime, buy 1,000 MCI at 5½. Now let's talk about your industry.
Broker: Brokerage stocks?
Schwartz: Remember we got rich on Coldwell Banker from '75 to '78, and the reason was the real estate boom. I think the market's going to boom, and you guys will be hitting 50- and 60-million-share-volume days. May even hit 100 million in another year.
Broker: Well, we're all four times earnings. I hear the possibility of over $4 earnings for Shearson. Your Open-Air says if Coldwell Banker stock can triple from 1975 to 1978 because of the real estate boom, then brokerage stocks will do the same because of a stock market boom.
Schwartz: Precisely. Get me 500 Shearson. What's the price?
Broker: 27. Now you won't feel so bad when you see the interest on your margin account.
Schwartz: How's the market anyway, and how are your incoming phone calls?
Broker: The Dow is now over 800. Very few incoming phone calls, and those are all asking about T-bills and our money market rates. It's mid-April; my gross is down; and brokers are all wondering what we're doing in this business. Everyone is looking for the next big down.
Schwartz: Great. All Open-Air buy signals. What's the score on those turkeys we bought?
Broker: They're all up except Ford. It's down a point.

⋘ 4 ⋙

OPEN-AIR ANALYSIS VERSUS OTHER MARKET APPROACHES

Computer, computer on the wall, who's the fairest stock of all?... But isn't that what everyone is buying?

To carve in stone one specific approach to the market will surely produce losses. Open-Air Analysis is the starting point, an overview, to be used when looking for money-making ideas. It's a detector, a Geiger counter, which, when put in motion, can incorporate additional methods of selecting and managing the investment. For instance, a stock might be uncovered using Open-Air Analysis and then be discarded after being run through the gauntlet of fundamentals, charts, and comparative analyses. Greyhound Corporation was a case in point. After the Arab oil embargo in 1973, it was obvious that more people would start riding the bus. Open-Air gave a signal, but on closer fundamental examination, Greyhound was found unattractive because of its meat-packing division, Armour.

"Don't buy anything over ten times earnings. If you're going to fall out of a building, it's better to fall out of the second or third floor rather than the tenth," advised one articulate "gnome" of North Dakota while being interviewed in his $40,000 tract home. There are as many approaches to the market as there are investors, and they come and go as fast as hot money managers.

Some contrarians say to stick with those areas that are overlooked: don't follow the crowd. Well, that means the contrarians did not participate in

> Concept stocks from 1968 to 1971
> The "nifty fifty" in 1972 and 1973
> Smokestack America coming out of the recession in 1975 and 1976
> Gambling stocks in 1977 and 1978
> Energy stocks in 1978, 1979, and 1980

So you see, Open-Air Analysis by definition observes trends and then translates those observations into the stock market. A movement has already started, and the crowd is forming. Therefore, an Open-Air investor could *not* possibly be a contrarian when it comes to individual stocks. Like a surfer, the Open-Air investor looks for the big wave and starts investing (paddling) ahead of it. Ride the big one all the way.

As illustrated in chapter two, being a contrarian can often produce profitable results when it comes to the total stock market direction, but where individual stock selection is concerned, it could lead you into the valley of do-nothing stocks. The contrarian might have successfully picked the market bottom in March 1980 and then decided to buy textiles as an overlooked group. Even when the big wave called "oil" became obvious, he refused to ride it, and went nowhere in the big 1980 market. So, the important point to distinguish here is that there are two different talents required and two different disciplines needed when

> Looking at the market
> Picking the stock

As we have discussed, Open-Air deals with both disciplines, but from different angles. What about selling? Like 100% Schwartz and the bowling alleys, we use the same

Geiger counter for a sell signal. Everything in between is managing the position. It's not enough to be a good stock picker; there are about six more challenging requirements while you own it. Like Terry Tomorrow, who conquered impatience in the holding of Rolm, only to sell it at 6 on the way to 40, the investor's work only begins once the stock is selected. These are six constant decisions always with you once you have bought a stock:

1. Realizing you're wrong and selling it.
2. Knowing when to hold it in the face of a weak stock market.
3. Knowing when to average down or up on existing holdings—and having the courage to do so.
4. Knowing when to sell it.
5. Realizing you may have sold too soon and having the perception to buy back the same stock even at a higher price.
6. Properly evaluating your holding when "it is doing nothing."

Within this framework, let's examine other investment approaches that might be used in harmony (or disharmony) with Open-Air Analysis.

Buy a stock when it first breaks into new highs. This is a good one! In fact, the charts below showing the first few stocks to break into the new high list after the March 27, 1980, Bunker Hunt lows will start you salivating. After a severe decline, it is meaningful to watch for the first new highs. Conversely, after a long upsurge, it is equally important to note the first new lows in a downturn after that long upsurge. Let's review how this worked coming out of "Silver Thursday," or the 180-point, six-week decline ending on March 27. The charts below show the respective new highs, and you will see what their prices were just a few months later, on August 7.

This is a proven approach. It doesn't work every time; a stock may make a new high suddenly because it's a take-over candidate, and when the courting period is over, it collapses. But for these stocks the results were phenomenal.

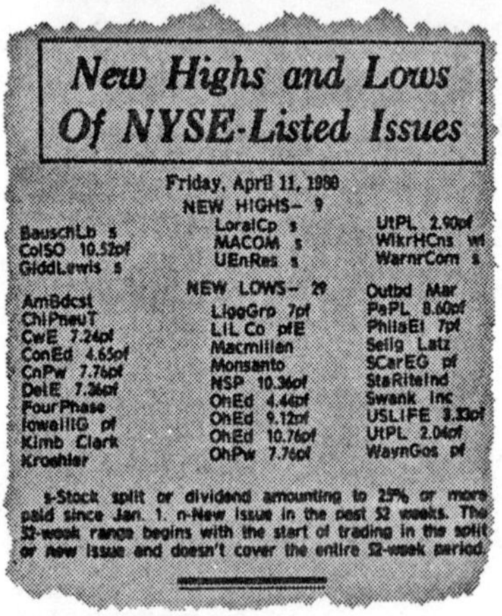

	CLOSES ON AUGUST 7, 1980	%
MA/COM	40	+55
Bausch & Lomb	55⅛	+36
Giddings & Lewis	33	+45
Loral	32	+20
Warner Communications	49	+17

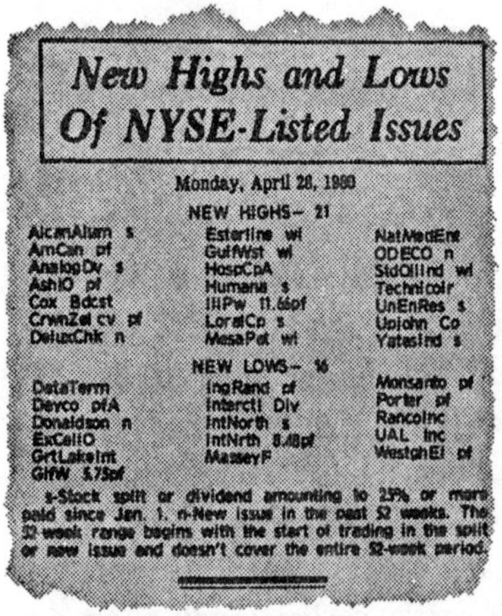

	CLOSES ON AUGUST 7, 1980	%
Alcan Aluminum	33⅝	+22
Cox Broadcasting	45¼	+45
Deluxe Check	45¼	+28
Gulf & Western	18	+20
Hospital Corporation	45	+28
Humana	55¼	+30
Mesa Petroleum	38¾	+40
National Medical Enterprises	45¾	+45
Sedco	51	+5
Standard Oil of Indiana	58½	+16
Technicolor	36½	+10
Upjohn	60	+25

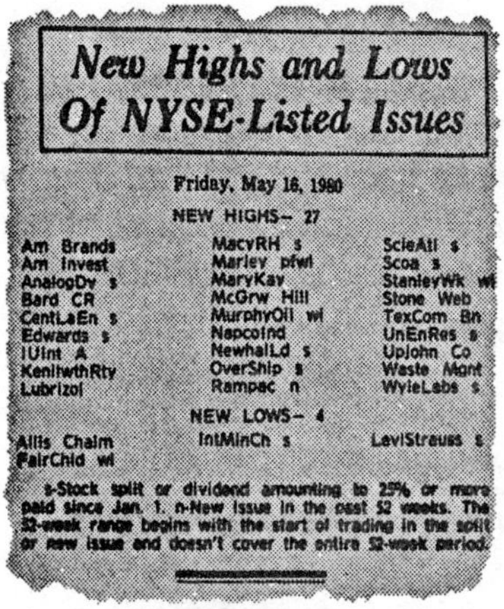

CLOSES ON AUGUST 7, 1980	%
American Brands 84	+12
Analog Devices 30¼	+80
Bard (C.R.) Inc. 19¼	+10
Kenilworth Realty 38¾	+ 8
Lubrizol Corporation 73⅝	+10
Macy 49¼	+40
Mary Kay 24⅞	+50
McGraw-Hill 36⅝	+20
Murphy Oil 35⅜	+21
Napco 20⅞	+50
Newhall Land 28¾	+40
Overseas Shipholding 32⅛	+31
Scientific Atlanta 38	+60
SCOA 24⅜	+20
Stanley Works 19⅝	+22
Stone & Webster 72⅞	+21
Waste Management 66¾	+45
Wyle Labs 15⅜	+40

Put in stop orders 10% under so you won't have big losses. Losers use this approach. This only makes sense after you've had a big gain in a stock, and its momentum, while still strong, has carried it past your target of being fully priced.

Concentrate on turn-around situations. Where do you turn around Chrysler, at 15 or 7? The key here is probably to wait until evidence is in that it has in fact turned around. Evidence is generally in the form of the first increase in earnings. Make sure those earnings are "operating income" earnings, otherwise you could be sucked into an earnings increase that is "nonrecurring": the company may have sold a building or a division. Also, you might weather the turnaround at a low price range only to be finished in time for a bear market.

Buy only stocks with underlying options. In case of down markets, you can write calls and cut your losses. This is a classic example of buying a stock for the wrong reason. A winner sees the green and the loser sees the sand traps. The razzle-dazzle of options, interest rate futures, spreads, straddles, and shorting will not be discussed here. You don't become a good tennis player by concentrating on the drop shot and top-spin lob. They can be used sparingly and at the right time are effective, but Bjorn Borg did not win five Wimbledons on razzle-dazzle.

Go for the total return; buy only stocks with big dividends. If you get a 7% dividend plus a 10% capital gain, that's 17% and is ahead of inflation. This sounds good to the investor who has had poor performance in his portfolio. But this approach would have eliminated the really big winners of the last three or four years—many of whom had only token dividends of 2 or 3% or none at all. These include stocks like

> Commodore International
> Computervision
> ISC Systems
> MA/COM
> MCI Communications
> Mark Products
> Petro Lewis
> Rolm
> Shearson Loeb Rhoades
> Tandy
> Teledyne
> Tom Brown

Henry Singleton, chief executive officer of Teledyne, had this to say about dividends: "Any company with debt that also pays a dividend is, in effect, borrowing to pay the dividend."

Dividends have an interesting history. Consider the following:

> GM cut its dividend in February 1975 from 3.40 to 2.40. One year later the stock had risen from 35 to 78.
> Again on May 6, 1980, GM cut the dividend. On May 5, the stock was 41½. By August 7, it was 53.
> The airlines totally omitted most of their dividends in the first quarter of 1980, which turned out to be their low point.

In fact, the entire picture of going after income (interest on dividends) vs. growth can be summarized in the following statement. In the five years ending in 1979, the Standard & Poor's 500 had an average annual total return (dividends plus capital appreciation) of 15% versus 8% for AAA corporate bonds and 7% for treasury bonds. Unfortunately, most investors seeking safety and high income in the last five years have suffered a loss of principal. Bonds and utilities through the spring of 1981 fared poorly. When interest rates stay high bonds and utilities stay low—it's that simple.

Four disciplines that won't fail:

1. Always take investment advice from people who are one of two types: those who have made it themselves or those who are experienced. They might have even experienced making it and then losing it. And, if you are taking advice from that someone who has made it, inquire who his or her broker or investment counselor is. It could be you're listening to Gary Gloryhog when the real pro is Betty Background.

2. It sounds basic, but know everything you can about the stock you own and its industry. The secret to discipline is knowing what to do in down markets. Should you get out

or buy more or ride it through? When you have bought stocks on tips from Benny Buy-Out, it's funny that he disappears when the stock tanks. Actually, it is in the down markets that you lay the groundwork for future profits. In down markets several things come into focus:

> Your own do-it-yourself analysis is not so good.
> Your broker is good or bad.
> You can't handle it.
> You notice the stocks that resist the downtrend.

So, what does knowing all about your company really mean?

- Get Value Line and Standard & Poor's sheets on the company in which you are interested.
- There is something wrong with every good idea, but know in advance what it is. The company could be heavily dependent on one customer or have labor negotiations coming up.
- Have your broker establish a contact at the company or, if this is impractical, have him ask them to send a copy of their 10-K for study.
- Call the retailers who carry your company's products and find out how they are doing. At the same time, inquire how the competitors are doing.
- Know when your company is due to report earnings, and then watch it carefully as it approaches that date. The *Stock Trader's Almanac* or most Standard & Poor's sheets divulge this information.
- Be aware of danger signals like late reporting by companies, and your broker not having his phone calls answered by your company. Corporate officers establish a reputation on Wall

Street. The "hypers" talk to analysts and brokers during good times, but won't return calls if something has gone wrong.

If your brokerage firm has recommended the stock, make sure you hear about all the comments from their research department.

3. The third discipline is never to get in and out of individual stocks because of the condition of the *market*. Get in and out of *stocks*! The enemy of Open-Air Analysis is the market. Markets can cause margin calls, but stocks can wipe you out. Markets can go up, but it's the individual stock that makes it big.

There is an old saying that there is more anxiety caused by being *out* of the market when it is going up than there is in being *in* the market while it is going down. Take the case of Marilyn Market Watcher. She got out of the market completely one week before Bunker Hunt day. It never seems to fail that wholesale liquidation generally occurs at or near the bottom, but Marilyn was happy and so was her broker, who had an excellent reputation, especially as a market technician. They laughed smugly at the disaster occurring, and the broker only wished he had gotten more clients entirely out. Here was a progression of their thought processes after they sold:

The stocks they sold *must* go down substantially to justify what they just did.

The broker, even if he feels otherwise, must wait a decent period before going back to his client and saying, "Get back in," or it will look like he is churning.

They both start doubting each rally and become members of the "next leg down bunch."

The broker's *first*-choice stocks start moving beyond buy points, forcing him into "second choices."

Marilyn becomes more anxious. Finally, since being out of the market is causing a strain between them, they throw abandon to the wind and jump back in—usually right before the next good-sized correction.

Remember, of the two important factors—the right stock and the right time in the market—the most important is the right stock. You can buy the right stock at the wrong time and be bailed out, but being in the wrong stock, even at the right time, can be long and agonizing. Have you noticed that money managers of large mutual funds are always referred to as being 20% or 30% in cash or fully invested, but *never* 100% in cash? They were not fully in cash even when money market funds were paying 17% in March and April of 1980.

4. The last discipline tip is to not get hung up on labels. A conversation to prove the point:

"Now, I want something that is 'A' rated. Here is a list of things my lawyer says might be good for growth potential."

"Is your lawyer an investment man? Does he manage money?" I asked.

"No, but he is a lawyer and smart as hell. He got me and my family out of several jams, and here is his list of what I should buy."

The list read:
Buy 300 Ford @ 42
Buy 400 Polaroid @ 51
Buy 400 EK @ 65
Buy 200 IBM @ 70
Buy 500 U. S. Steel @ 26
Buy 500 Goodyear @ 17
Buy 500 Firestone @ 13
Buy 800 Sears @ 20

It was spring 1979.

> "Well, those are great companies, but sometimes companies mature, and they only move when there are great bull markets. You might consider emerging companies that can grow on their own. Stocks like:
> Digital Equipment @ 50
> Merrill Lynch @ 19
> Teledyne @ 90
> Computervision @ 12
> Barry Wright @ 16
> Wainoco Oil @ 11
> Rolm @ 8
> Scientific Atlanta @ 13
> Humana @ 22

> "Those are all speculations. I've never heard of the damn things. Go ahead and buy my attorney's list."

We find security in names and labels and treat yesterday's giants with reverence. For drill, let's see how the "label" list fared going through the bad markets of October 1979 and March 1980 compared with the so-called speculation list.

	ON "BUY DATE"	ON AUGUST 30, 1980
LABEL LIST		
Ford	42	27⅜
Polaroid	51	27¾
EK	65	64¼
IBM	70	65½
U. S. Steel	26	22⅝
Goodyear	17	15⅞
Firestone	13	8
Sears	20	17½

	ON "BUY DATE"	ON AUGUST 30, 1980
SPECULATIVE LIST		
Digital Equipment	50	85½
Merrill Lynch	19	30¼
Teledyne	90	165
Computervision	12	45⅝
Barry Wright	16	37½
Wainoco Oil	11	36¾
Rolm	8	36⅛
Scientific Atlanta	13	38½
Humana	22	53¼

Moral of the story: use investment people for investment advice and lawyers for legal advice.

In summary, while you need to perfect Open-Air Analysis, you must also have discipline. After you have acquired the discipline, you can then, in teamwork with your broker, incorporate the other types of approaches. Not every stock is an Open-Air. However, incorporating other approaches with Open-Air is necessary for complete analysis. Choosing that appropriate "other" approach is crucial. For instance, watching the new high and low list can reveal an Open-Air stock. Placing 10% stops under stocks is the mechanical reflex of a loser.

Broker: This market is getting to me. I'm so preoccupied I got up and took two showers this morning. I'm listening to news all the time and read like crazy. I've got plenty of time, because I can't get people to buy anything, and the incoming phone calls are all from other brokers.

Schwartz: Best signs in the world. Just keep buying.
Broker: Which is why you're buying now. By the way, are you aware of the money supply figures? On May 8 they were down another $3 billion. That brings the Fed down to a money supply rate of 2% in the last three weeks, and their target is 6% to 7%. So there's plenty of room still to expand the money supply. The Bo Dereks 11¾% of 2010 are now 115$^{17}/_{32}$ and 90-day T-bills are 9%.
Schwartz: T-bills have come down from 16½ to 9% in five weeks: that's unbelievable! Remember, it took about nine months for interest rates to fall that far in 1975.
Broker: And the market went up almost 400 points. What does your "Open-Air" crystal ball say to you these days, 100%?
Schwartz: It's still saying "buy." But let me hit you with an Open-Air. If everyone is moving to the Sun Belt, why aren't we in some of the builders or retailers in that area? Even energy companies like Mesa Petroleum at 31, Murphy Oil at 81, Big Three at 45, Louisiana Land at 40, Union Pacific at 42½, and Tom Brown at 14⅞? Incidentally, you know I'm attracted to companies that buy their own stock. How come you never put me in Teledyne?
Broker: That's like what the jockey said when the owner asked him why he didn't go to the front. "Because that position was taken, sir." So, in answer to your question, every time we looked at Teledyne you were out of money.
Schwartz: Well, my Shearson's doing well. Have they finished buying up their own stock—a half-million shares?

Broker: Not yet. Let's talk some more about your Sun Belt package.

Schwartz: Okay, send me some information. It kind of puts me off to think of buying six stocks at once. It's an Open-Air, but let's take one at a time. In the meantime, what are the movers and shakers doing today?

Broker: What we do best—anything to frustrate the average investor.

Schwartz: We're now up over 850 while everyone is still looking for another big down. Remember, the first 100 points are doubted.

Broker: It's called climbing a wall of worry.

Schwartz: The crowd is in cash. Show me a person waiting for a correction and I'll show you someone who got blown out around Bunker Hunt day and never got back in. Buy into disaster, my boy.

Broker: Well, let's buy a Chrysler dealership, and property at the foot of Mount St. Helens.

Schwartz: Smart ass! How come you never got me into Kirby Petroleum? It was 46 on Bunker Hunt day and yesterday hit 80. Also, how much of that new issue Magnuson Computer did you get me?

Broker: I put in for 4,000 shares and got 500. You can have 200 at the offering price of 20.

Schwartz: Who gets the rest . . . Mom, Dad, and Aunt Jane?

Broker: That's 40% of everything I got, and you only make up 10% of my gross. Give me a break.

Schwartz: Okay, give me some quotes. I own so many goddamn stocks lately I can't keep track.

Broker: Shearson is 28¾. MCI Communications is 7¾. Ford is 25¼. Juniper is 14. Tony Lama is 9. Eastman Kodak is 53½. Magnuson is already up

2½ from the offering. Standard of Indiana is 51½ after a 2 for 1, and Standard of Ohio is 94 but also splitting 2 for 1. Knogo is 15¼ after a split, and Sensormatic is 31.

Schwartz: Well, I'm up on all but one—Ford. Any news on Ford?

Broker: You're talking like a client again, wanting to talk about the one that's down—never satisfied. Can you believe this story: I put a lady into 1,000 MCI at 5 and she called me at 7 and said, "What's going on?" like it wasn't supposed to move.

Schwartz: Oh, you live in the fast lane of life. By the way, what do you know about a company called Minnetonka?

Broker: Never heard of it.

Schwartz: I was in a store the other day, and my wife bought this new liquid soap called Softsoap. Have you seen it? It's got a dispenser and you press down; you need no soap dishes, and the stuff smells terrific. I don't see anyone else with the same product, and can you visualize the market for this stuff? Open-Air, Open-Air! Every home, doctor's office, business office—my god!

Broker: Minnetonka is 8. It has a small sales base, so one big product like this could have an impact if it goes. The earnings record is a winner and the P/E is about 12, but those earnings are growing at about 30%. You're right, a real Open-Air, but how long will Procter & Gamble and Colgate let a pipsqueak company take part of their business?

Schwartz: About as long as IBM allowed Prime Computer

and Computervision. Look, it's not a slam-dunk... more like a jump shot from half court at the buzzer. But the store owner said she was selling it as fast as it came in. I'm going to check some markets and drugstores. Let's take a peep and buy 200 for drill.

Broker: How do you like the market?

Schwartz: Love it. That's why I'm not considering diversifying yet and not even thinking about taking profits.

Broker: The full court press. And what if you're wrong? We don't know tops and bottoms when we're looking at them. Maybe we're looking at one now.

Schwartz: This is me you're talking to. We've been through '74 and '75, the Octobers of '78 and '79, and this last deal. Look, there's a new awareness in this country. The start of the cure is the first sign of the pain. And man, this country has had pain. As a result, it understands economics better—even Congress is starting to shape up. A capitalistic stirring is beginning. I firmly believe that the eighties could be like the sixties.

Broker: Regardless of who gets in?

Schwartz: That's right, although Reagan might whip inflation faster.

Broker: I'm just concerned you're getting over $200,000 in eight or nine issues on the way up and then when it starts down, some event like war in the Middle East blows you out with a margin call, and everything we've accomplished goes down the drain.

Schwartz: Come on, give me a break. You know we learned that lesson a long time ago.

Broker: What lesson?

Schwartz: You never panic because of a market, only because of an individual stock. I panicked when Itel's trouble first started appearing. True, I took a loss, and the stock had already fallen from 35 to 20, but that's better than 4! Check on Minnetonka and those others, and call me.

⦅ 5 ⦆

MY BROKER MAKE ME DO IT

(ARE BROKERS WORTH IT?)

Broker: Schwartz, what do you want in a stockbroker?
Schwartz: I want a broker who will make me do it! But I can't have the feeling he's just selling me.
Broker: Making you do it means selling you.
Schwartz: Look, after you've been with a broker through six or seven trades and a couple of sharp corrections, you can tell whether you've got a broker or a salesman. You can also tell whether you have a service broker or a control broker.
Broker: Control?
Schwartz: Yes. Someone who wants to call all of the shots and have you follow.
Broker: Which do you prefer?
Schwartz: I prefer the one who at least has enough confidence in himself to want to call all the shots. Hell, anyone can read me wires from New York. Order-taker types flood you with information and wait for your decision.
Broker: Sometimes it takes us a while to gain a client's confidence, so we send supporting evidence of what we believe.

Schwartz: Don't get me wrong; I need all of that stuff, but I would hope the broker would send me material that he has already screened—even material he might not be interested in, but knows I am. I have to believe that brokerage firm analysts making $150,000 a year ought to make me some money, and the only access I have to them is through my broker.

Broker: Well, do you make your own selections or follow the broker?

Schwartz: That's my point. It's both! I'm looking to get "married" to someone I can trust and who understands how I think. In fact, who thinks like I do. You know, Open-Airs. I want a financial doubles team, with a partner smarter than I am about the market.

Broker: You mean the broker must be good at market timing, and you pick the stocks?

Schwartz: No! Let me finish. I want not just anyone who can explain margin and balance sheets and income statements, but someone who can interpret news and how it will affect my stocks. I want someone willing to call the company or the analyst, if necessary. Also, someone who won't mind if I call him at home if it's urgent.

Broker: You want all that and probably 30% commission discounts.

Schwartz: We'll have another discussion on that subject.

Broker: Okay. What do you want to accomplish with your account?

Schwartz: I'm in the market to make money. No fancy names like capital appreciation or total return. If I were sixty-five with a portfolio of $250,000, then you could dazzle me with safety, income, bonds, diversification and all that money management garbage. Maybe if I were fifty-five, I might be satisfied with staying ahead of inflation—like 20% a year, dividends and capital gains combined. But I'm forty-five, make a good income, and I've got $250,000 worth of stock that I want to be worth a couple of mil by the time I'm sixty.

Broker: That means you're willing to speculate. You could wind up with $50,000!

Schwartz: Hey, you're about to disqualify yourself! I want a broker who *believes* it can be done, has experienced other clients doing it, and who appreciates the risks involved. What's more important, I want a broker who is in the market himself.

Broker: How many brokers have you had? At first, it sounded like you were auditioning for a couple of years.

Schwartz: Four: one woman and three men. I had success and failure with all of them, but I know *my* weaknesses. I can spot trends and analyze, but I need my broker to make me do it without his having to be right and deal only in his stocks.

Broker: Well, I'm now a veteran in this business, and as you know, I also trade my own account. In fact, it's also my goal to make a million. I believe a broker not making money in his own account is like a dentist having bad gums. Or, it might be like a real estate agent in the seventies not buying any property for himself.

Schwartz: One of the top money managers in Wall Street used only to hire analysts who had an experience of at least one of their recommendations going into bankruptcy. I like my brokers to have been through good and bad markets. You've earned your ticker tape going through October '78 and '79 and Bunker Hunt day.

Broker: Why do they call you 100%?

Schwartz: Because I finish in the black every year. I've had my losses, but I've only had one losing year, 1974. Some years have been big like '75 and '78 when my net worth was up 60%. Other years, like '77 and '79, I was only up 20%. 1980 is not over yet, but I'm doing fine. Incidentally, I don't figure dividends.

Broker: Then why did you keep changing brokers?

Schwartz: I was still looking for that personality who could make me a million. Not all brokers think big you know, and...

Broker: Open-Air says, just when you start thinking too big, it's time to get out.

Schwartz: True, if you think big, it's better at bottoms than at tops, but first you've got to demonstrate that you can even think big at all. If I want to put my $250,000 into three stocks, some brokers are terrorized. I know they are looking out for my best interests, but a broker should be flexible. A client who wants to make a million can't afford a broker who thinks about yield.

Broker: What are you most comfortable with—picking your own stocks or having the broker pick the stocks?

Schwartz: If I pick a stock, it's probably because the broker has worked with me and gotten the background. I don't want to feel he's not rooting for me just because it wasn't *his* stock.

Broker: Yes, but the getting-acquainted period between client and broker can be costly. I have an account in which the first four trades we made (all my ideas) were losses. Then we more than made it up. He stuck with me and hasn't had a losing year since '78.

Schwartz: Look, it's not enough to pick winners. The broker has to show me that he or she can make me do it, make me hang on or buy more when it drops or, finally, sell. It's no relationship when the broker picks Itel at 12 and it goes to 30 and then he feels his job is over, leaving it up to me to call the sale. All of a sudden I become Larry Long-Term and the son-of-a-bitch goes to 2. Really, I'm longing for that feeling of confidence to the point where I'll go along 100% with him.

Broker: And you only get that after thick and thin and mostly going through bad markets.

Schwartz: Incidentally, how many clients do you have?

Broker: About 300.

Schwartz: What's the largest?

Broker: Market value 1½ million.

Schwartz: So, at least large accounts don't frighten you.

Broker: I'd rather have a large one than a small one.

Schwartz: Do you do commodities, options, and tax shelters?

Broker: As for options, you've heard the expression that profitable options are held twenty-four hours, and unprofitable ones are held to expiration? I do very little option business.

Schwartz: Why?

Broker: Options are not really a portfolio-building strategy, they're more a temporary improvement on a rate of return. As for commodities, they say if you want to make a *small* fortune, then start with a *large* one. I can't do justice to my stock clients if I'm handling commodities. Besides, our

	guys in New York have had great records with their managed commodity portfolios. I turn it over to them.
Schwartz:	Hey, philosophy never made me any money. Open-Air has, so let's get back to business. What about that MA/COM?
Broker:	Well, the stock is now 30, up from 21, but I talked to their director of investor relations, and it really looks like a winner. They have acquired several companies and have become a leader in the manufacture of telecommunications equipment. They cover the range from voice to light frequencies. It puts them into satellite and data communications, cable TV and defense telecommunications.
Schwartz:	How do you compare this to Rolm?
Broker:	Rolm is in a specific niche of telecommunications. MA/COM manufactures microwave components for the entire industry. It's growing at 25% a year and sells for a P/E *below* Rolm.
Schwartz:	Okay, let's pick up 500. How about Minnetonka? Every store I talk to says they can't keep Softsoap in stock. Liquid soap containers in all the homes and offices—that's a huge market.
Broker:	Until P&G and Colgate come pouring in. Although they do have a great balance sheet.
Schwartz:	You know the advantage of being first. Let's get another 800. What's the price?
Broker:	It's up to 12. You paid 8 last week.
Schwartz:	12! Why the hell didn't you tell me? You're not really sold, are you? If this company can earn $1.25 next year and if it can sell at 15 times earnings on 30% to 40% growth rates, then it should double. Go ahead.
Broker:	It's just that I've seen this type of thing have a

short life. Even your Rival Crock-Pot didn't last forever.
Schwartz: Just long enough to make a ton.
Broker: Done.

What are some of the complaints about brokers?

1. "My broker never tells me to sell."
2. "I get the feeling he is churning my account for the commissions."
3. "If there is a big drop, as in October 1978 and March 1980, he makes out both ways."
4. "I go in to see her and it's like visiting someone who keeps the TV on. She's always looking at that screen or answering the telephone."
5. "I'm intimidated. I don't know anything about the market, and she's always putting me on hold. She always seems too busy."
6. "He recommends a stock, it drops 20% and then I get 'We don't follow it anymore.'"
7. "When markets get bad, I have to cheer him up."

Are these legitimate complaints? *Yes!* And furthermore, brokers you deal with over the years are probably going to qualify for all of these complaints at one time or another. *What sort of person is this broker?*

A broker in the business at least five years has about 250 clients. Of these, around 20% give him 80% of his commission income business. A broker's advice can reflect the year he or she entered the business. For instance, a broker entering the business in the seventies did not experience long, sustained bull markets. In order to make money for clients in the seventies, a broker had to be agile and, consequently, became short-term "sell" oriented. So when a broker might appear to want to "churn," the truth of the matter is that he probably lacks conviction about the long term because he hasn't experienced it. He is a 1970-oriented broker.

Also, these brokers have been through a general period of rising interest rates, so they have witnessed falling bond prices and falling utility prices. In short, the broker of the seventies turned to options, tax shelters, commodities, annuities, and very short swings in stocks. These have been "ports in a storm." So it is well to know how long a broker has been in the business and during which years. Ask! The conditions of a broker's baptism reflect the advice you are given.

Conversely, the broker who went through the fifties and sixties saw fortunes made in the stock market and generally still thinks more long-term. In fact, because of the sixties, a broker may be guilty of the complaint, "He never tells me to sell."

What about the relationship between stockbrokers and brokerage firms? Is it true brokerage firms never say "sell"? Not anymore! Sometimes, however, they do employ subtle recommendations like: "Sears has been reduced from a buy to a hold." Around the trade that could mean, "Hold it for the long term while it falls from 25 to 15." Next time someone says he is a long-term investor, it might be some poor soul who never got a "sell" suggestion. Or he got one and ignored it. It would be wise to determine what kind of broker you have, and how forceful are his or her firm's sell suggestions.

Because brokerage firms can't follow every publicly held company available, they try to reduce the size to ones that lend themselves to constant supervision, believing that a company closely followed has a better chance for investment success. The broker who follows his firm exclusively might miss some dramatic winners, but the trade-off is being able to detect trouble in time and avoid disaster.

The broker who, in addition to following his firm, also shows a willingness to venture out into uncharted waters does so with several caveats involved:

He must be confident of his own analysis.
He must be confident of his own sources of information.
He generally brings this stock to the attention of old reliable and loyal clients.

Stockbrokers have big egos. Some want to land in the stockbrokers' Hall of Fame. What keeps them going is picking more winners than losers.

Is your broker worth it? If he isn't, fire him! (See chapter nine.) You are there to make money. Most other considerations are secondary, yet it is amazing how many clients stay with someone who has not made them money. After two years and no gain in net worth, it's time for a change.

What do brokers think about their fellow brokers? "If a broker knew he was going to die, how many of his associates in the office would he advise his wife to consult?" and "Who in the office would he let handle his mother's account?" are good questions. However, it's horses for courses. There are brokers good at stocks and others good at commodities; some are good speculators, and others are conservative. A young, probing, money-making broker might not be suitable for your wife or mother, but might be perfect for a risk-taker. Some brokers are great in up markets and lousy in down markets and vice versa. Sometimes a broker's actions will give you a clue to when to buy or sell. One client would start selling when his broker took long lunches at fancy restaurants. Conversely, he would buy when he found the broker bringing his lunch to the office.

Brokers can be therapy. For no charge they can also provide information that will be invaluable to your own business or personal planning. Having access to economic predictions and reports of interest rates can provide valuable lead-time advantages for your own business planning. You can't talk to your doctor or attorney once a week about politics, current events, or sociological changes. Indirectly, your broker can help in the purchase of a house, car, or furniture; these are economic stories he lives with every day.

There are fair-weather brokers just like clients. As one veteran put it, "Down markets eliminate the order-takers from the stockbrokers." You can tell a lot about brokers and clients during down markets.

If your broker has done well for you, follow him. Why leave a winner? If the results have been mediocre, then either stay in the same firm and try another person in the same branch office, or try out someone who has been interested in getting your business. (Always consider your results versus the market. Don't demand that a broker make you 25% in a year when the market is down 20%.)

On the subject of brokerage firms, the following list gives the top twenty firms, according to total capital, at the end of 1980.*

1. Merrill Lynch
2. Shearson Loeb Rhoades (now Shearson American Express)
3. E. F. Hutton
4. Paine Webber
5. Salomon Brothers
6. Dean Witter Reynolds
7. Goldman Sachs
8. Bache Halsey Stuart Shields
9. Stephens, Inc.
10. First Boston
11. Morgan Stanley
12. Drexel Burnham Lambert
13. Allen and Company
14. Lehman Brothers, Kuhn Loeb

---

* *Institutional Investor* magazine.

15. Kidder, Peabody and Company
16. Donaldson, Lufkin and Jenrette
17. A. G. Becker-Warburg
18. Shelbey, Cullom, Dorn and Company
19. Bear Stearns
20. Smith Barney Harris Upham

6

CAN YOUR STOCKBROKER FIND HAPPINESS WITH OPEN-AIR?

(DOES THE COMMISSION SYSTEM WORK AGAINST YOUR PROFITS?)

"How in the hell can I exercise patience and Open-Air Analysis in managing money for clients when I have to make a living every day?" exhorts a broker during the 200-point rally from April to July of 1980. "I hold their hands on the way down and don't get paid. Can't get them in at the bottom and don't get paid. The market turns up and now they're making money, but I haven't made a dime."

"Look, everybody wins—my clients have some profits and I'll have some gross. If we tank and go down 100 points they say, 'How come you never told me to sell?' If I take them out now with 30 or 40% profits, and the Dow goes to 1,000, then they call me Charlie Churn-em." The constant dilemma of a stockbroker! What if *brokers* were on salary? Does the commission system work for them and against you?

One way to answer the first question is to go back and evaluate the performance of money managers who are on salary. As you will see in chapter nine, the performance of pooled equity funds from 1975 through 1979 did not match the Standard & Poor's average. Perhaps a person on salary lacks the initiative to perform. After all, the broker is totally dependent upon the customer for a livelihood. If the broker does not perform, the customer leaves. That's plenty of incentive. Surprisingly, the least active investors are the ones most concerned with commissions.

Secondly, the commission causes the broker to make you do it! True, he might make you lose, but if a broker does have the pressure of commissions, he does *not* have the pressure of bad advice. On the contrary, if he gets a commission on anything he sells to you, then why not choose the best idea?

Down markets can often accomplish one favor for the investing public: they give the brokerage firm a cleansing. Flushed out of the business are the hot salesmen and Charlie Churn-ems, because prolonged bad performance makes an ex-stockbroker. Maybe the whole world would be better off on the commission system, because it certainly reveals who is productive.

Obviously, the broker overcomes the pressure of commission the same way any business does—by expanding clientele. Since a broker's clientele expands largely through referrals, it all goes back to performance.

But what happens to the broker's objectivity in bad markets? Isn't he forced into selling what's easy? For example, in times of fear and uncertainty when stock prices are down, brokers recommend utilities and bond funds (with higher mark-ups) rather than depressed growth stocks or blue chips. Isn't this a case where the pressure of commission causes the broker to go the wrong way? True, but once again, he often takes the "easy sell" largely because clients, being human beings, are frightened to death at bottoms and want nothing to do with Computervision at 15 down from 25, or Tandy at 25 down from 35, or MA/COM at 10 down from 18, or Teledyne at 78 down from 100. Unfortunately, the broker who is still regarded as "a salesman" by his client finds himself in the frustrated position of being unable to convince people to buy stocks at bottoms, so in order to make a living, he tells people what they want to hear: "You can't go wrong with a little Niagara Mohawk down 10 points from its high and yielding 12%."

The broker and client who have been through the storms together both tend to recognize when the risk/reward ratios are in their favor. The difference is that the client knows he is not being "sold"... because they've made these moves before.

So, how can a rookie broker even begin to practice anything like Open-Air Analysis while building a clientele? It isn't easy, unless he's a rookie broker with a wealthy family as a client. A rookie has been trained to build the business, to forget about being an analyst, and to follow the firm's recommendations. It's not all bad. He becomes Sidney Service, and this works very well with certain clients.

If the feeling persists that your broker is more interested in commissions than he is in making you money, there are several ways to tell if his recommendations are being influenced by conviction or commission.

> Does he keep recommending a new stock each time he calls?
> If he suggests selling Dome Petroleum and it goes up two points, does he suggest selling it again?
> Do you hate to call him just for a check on things because he just "sells" all the time?
> If you bought Gulf Oil on his suggestion at 40 and it's now 35, does he say buy more?
> Does he recommend stocks like GM, Exxon, IBM, Du Pont, Eastman Kodak, or American Brands—stocks which he knows you will not likely sell?
> Does he concentrate on high mark-up products like mutual funds? Remember, if a broker is commission-hungry and recommends that you put your $10,000 in a mutual fund with a 6% or $600 commission (of which he gets $300), he is saying "bye-bye" to

that money. On buying and selling stocks with $10,000, he might make ten round-turn trades over a two-year period and take in $1,500 in commissions from which he could make $600.

Are you part of his EOM crowd? "End of the month" for most brokerage firms' accounting is generally the last trading day that allows five business days to settle. So, if you *always* get calls on the 23rd, 24th, or 25th of the month, he may be struggling to make a draw or cross some breakpoint in the commission matrix.

HOW MUCH MONEY DO BROKERS MAKE AND HOW ARE THEY PAID?

A recent check with the five leading brokerage firms indicates that the average broker in 1980 made $45–$50,000. According to *Fortune* magazine, over a hundred brokers grossed in excess of $1 million, the highest reported figure being $2.5 million.

Brokers get approximately 32% or 35% of their gross commissions. As they progress up the matrix and once they reach $100,000 in commissions, they could be making 40%. So, if you have given your broker $1,000 worth of gross commissions in a year, he will net for himself, before taxes, around $350. Within the total commission framework, there are generally several schedules. For instance, a broker might make 35% on stocks listed on the New York Stock Exchange, 40% on over-the-counter, 40% on underwritings, and 50% on mutual funds.

Remember, getting money under management is as important to brokers as it is to banks, savings and loans, insurance companies or investment counselors. The more money under management, the more business for the broker.

CONTESTS AND INTERNAL RECOGNITION FOR BIG PRODUCERS

Who benefits, you or the broker?

"I'm at $170,000 and it's July. I've got to get to $250,000 so I can make the President's Club and go to Hawaii. We've had a 200-point move, and still the phones don't ring. I can't get anyone to do anything," sighs a frustrated big hitter who makes $100,000 a year.

Do his recommendations have your interests at heart, or his trip to Hawaii? In all organizations, there is recognition for the most successful. Is this any different? Where contests and recognition are concerned, the broker's commission business is rewarded, but what about his client's performance?

Some frank answers to this question by actual brokers:

"Just because I do a lot of business doesn't mean my clients suffer. In fact, it's probably the reverse. If I'm doing a lot of business, it's because I handle larger accounts. If I handle larger accounts, I'm dealing with more sophisticated people—people who feed me information. Big producers are good catalysts of information between a broker and his clientele, and all should therefore participate."

"That's stupid! If I'm going to give bad advice, it won't be because a contest is on that might represent 10% of my entire income."

"I remember when I had just a few hundred dollars to go to make $20,000 a month for the first time. It meant a pair of diamond cuff links worth about $1,000. I put a small client into MCI Communications at 3 on the last day to qualify. MCI is now 14, and we both won!"

One active client suggests:

"They pass out sheets so each broker in the office knows where he stands on the commission ladder. This creates the necessary peer group competition. As a client, I feel good about doing business with a large producer, providing he's making me money. In addition, I'd like to have branch offices pass out a sheet showing the best stock pickers. Keep inter-office contests going on stock selection. In the final analysis, that's the best peer group pressure."

THINGS BROKERS DO FOR FREE

You should be able to receive the latest information on all of their selections, which includes separate write-ups. In addition, most brokerage firm branch offices subscribe to Standard & Poor's and Value Line. Individual brokers often subscribe to outside investment advisory services in order to supplement their own research: services such as Trendline (charts), Professional Tape Reader, and Dow Theory. In addition, most branch offices have a hotline to New York on which analysts talk about their respective industries. Clients may come in and listen. So on a given stock, you should be able to have access to:

- A brokerage firm report (if they follow up)
- A Value Line or Standard & Poor's sheet
- An up-to-date wire reflecting a recent opinion on the stock by the brokerage firm
- Comments by outside advisory services
- A chart interpretation
- An interpretation by your broker
- A conference call about the company or its industry

Most brokerage firms provide monthly statements for street name accounts. Street name accounts are now widely used as a result of SIPC (Securities Investor Protection Corporation). This insures every account up to $300,000, but most firms increase that to $500,000. The monthly statement also acts as a mini-portfolio review. In addition, many firms provide complete portfolio reviews every three months for accounts over $50,000. Dividends are collected and mailed at least once a month, and a year-end tax statement is prepared. Money market transactions are done without commission. Keeping track of money market transactions can be very time consuming.

COMMISSION-FREE OFFERINGS:
NEW ISSUES AND SECONDARY ISSUES

In this instance the broker is saying to you that his commission is paid by the issuing corporation and not by you. In brokerage language it's referred to as "working the calendar." It is also called investment banking, and utilities are constant fund raisers. In simplistic terms, when interest rates are high, utilities are forced to sell common stock, which dilutes existing per-share earnings. A syndicate, composed of as many as thirty or forty brokerage firms and headed by a manager who underwrites the issue, offers the securities at a price to reflect the day's closing. If Middle South Utilities closed at 12½, the price to you would be 12½ or 12⅝ *net*—no commission.

Offerings can be available, oversubscribed, or subject. The word *oversubscribed* is another way of saying "hot." In other words, there are more orders than there are stocks or bonds for sale. In this instance, each branch office is allocated an amount generally reflective of its respective underwriting history. For instance, if an office does a large amount of underwriting, it will receive generous amounts of offerings. This becames all-important when it comes to new issues, which will be discussed shortly. Secondary issues are those stocks for which a market already exists.

"Subject" means you can get some only if there are cancellations.

If you are a loyal customer and on the broker's "first team," you can expect to reap the fruits of new issues. From a business standpoint, first team members are generally clients who have given their brokers the most commissions; or someone for whom the broker may want to do a favor. So, if Genentech or Apple Computer, for example, are new issues to the market and your broker gets 500 shares, he will probably give 100 shares each to his five biggest accounts. In the case of Genentech and Apple, it was quite unusual if brokers got any.

Brokers are not permitted to buy oversubscribed stocks or bonds for their own accounts or for members of their families. To do so is a violation of the New York Stock Exchange "free riding" rule. Incidentally, brokers and their families have special numbered accounts that are closely monitored.

The net commission to the broker on "commission free" deals is about the New York Stock Exchange equivalent, except that the broker's percentage will probably be 40% instead of 35% as on New York list stocks.

How well do new offerings perform?

	OFFERING PRICE	PRICE 6 MONTHS LATER
Magnuson Computer	20	31¼
General Defense	11	15⅝
Applicon	22	48¾
BancTec	16	24¾
Enzo Biochem	6¼	28
ISC Systems	19½	42½
Service Fracturing	15	33

Listed on the previous page is a random sampling of new issue offerings from the summer of 1980, a period of generally accelerated stock prices.

SELECTING BROKERS

Outside of most racetracks you can find touts. They pass out pink or yellow sheets with their picks of the day: long shot of the day, best bet of the day, sleeper. Are brokerage firms high-class touts? They wear pinstripe suits, and Ivy League analysts prepare thirty-page institutional reports so the retail broker can say, "Our oil analyst is about to recommend Patrick Petroleum. Better get on before the report comes out."

If they are high-class touts, what do they have to gain? Commissions! But, if Paine Webber happens to pick a few more winners than Merrill Lynch or E. F. Hutton while they are generating these commissions, then what happens? Merrill, Dean Witter, Shearson, and E. F. Hutton pay more money to get better "winner pickers." The net result is what competition generally affords everyone: better performance.

To the investor who has taken the recommendation of a brokerage firm only to have it become a big loser, it is small compensation to say that firms spend millions of dollars on research for the benefit of their clientele. The brokerage firms argue that you can't evaluate a firm on the basis of one selection or even an investing period of one year. Like baseball, the winner of the World Series has had some losers.

Some say the difference between E. F. Hutton and Dean Witter Reynolds is the individual broker with whom you do business. If that's true, why not try two brokers? The answer to this might be determined by two things: the size and activity of your account. If you're sixty-five years old, have

$20,000 in the market, and are seeking safety and income, it will probably work against you to split $20,000 between two brokers. If your account is $100,000 and your primary goal is capital gains, then it might work providing . . .

> You don't play one against the other
>
> You don't buy Broker A's recommendation through Broker B (Broker A knows more about the stock than B, and if news broke dictating an immediate contact with all his clients, you don't get called because A doesn't know you bought it from B)
>
> You let both brokers know you are doing this (On most new account applications, the broker has to indicate whether you are doing business with another firm anyway)

If you are open and honest about your reasons for having two brokers, then you will retain the brokers' loyalty. (One might be good in commodities and one in stocks, or one good at options and another at stocks.) Remember, the broker will be as loyal to you as you are to him.

There are examples of clients with $100,000 accounts who openly declare a contest between the two brokers. They give each of them $50,000, saying that after one year whoever has the best record gets the entire amount.

WHEN SHOULD YOU EXPECT A DISCOUNT?

When asked whether they would use a discount broker, clients say:

> "I wouldn't go to a discount broker any more than I'd send my kid to a discount orthodontist."
>
> "I would. Not only am I saving on commissions, but I'm saving on not getting all of that lousy advice."

"Who needs a broker? I take *Granville, The Professional Tape Reader*, read *Barron's, The Wall Street Journal*, and *Forbes*. In addition, I watch TV news and *Wall Street Week*. It costs me over $1,000 a year and a lot of time, but it's worth it."

Full service brokers say:

"I work very hard for my clients. When my doctor, lawyer, and dentist start discounting to me, then I'll do the same. This is an ongoing, everyday relationship between client and broker, not an after-Christmas sale at Macy's. You get what you pay for."

"Commissions are a cost of doing business. Most businesses treat their best customers with extra goodies and volume discounts. I do the same. Once a client has given me $2,000 in commissions, I give him 10% off. When he crosses $5,000 it's 15%. I don't go beyond that, because then my firm would start taking a percentage of my take-home."

Discount brokers say:

"Commissions lead the salesman to pressuring the investor with trades that aren't in his or her best interest. In fact, the higher the risk of the trade, the greater the commission, and this leads to a kind of adversary relationship."

Full-line brokerage firms do allow their brokers some latitude with respect to discounting. For instance, Merrill Lynch will give a 20% discount on a purchase if the total money is put up in advance. E. F. Hutton offers a 15% discount on the sell side if a customer sells within thirty days. Most brokers grant commission relief if stocks are bought and sold within thirty days. But since a broker might talk to his client four or five times before a commission is generated, he will be reluctant to grant a discount to someone who has already taken thirty minutes of conversation and another hour of research. Again, it depends on the size of the order and amount of activity by the client.

Discount brokers do not give you the discussion and research necessary to make consistently correct decisions. It is when our own individual stock is down, or when the market is very weak, that most of us really need that second opinion. Discount brokers very seldom make outgoing phone calls. It is often the outgoing phone call to a client after a market is down that "makes him do it." The discounters are not going to spend time discussing farm prices, foreign developments, the economy, or interest rates. They do offer minimum insurance protection and margin accounts, but do not provide portfolio reviews. At the last report, most discounters clear through larger brokerage firms, except for Shearson American Express and E. F. Hutton, who clear only for their own clients.

Approximately 8% of all stock trading business is done with discounters, but a significant part of that is one-time liquidations.

What about errors and bad executions? In May 1980 the largest discount brokerage firm was forced to cancel its plans for a public offering when it was learned that the firm had suffered costly back-office foul-ups. The firm was forced to use nearly 11% of total commission income to cover bad debts and execution errors! What saved one unfortunate discounter's profitability was the interest charged on margin accounts.

In contrast, the average error rate for all the New York Stock Exchange member firms is just 1.4%. Ironically, it was the heavy trading in active markets that created problems for the discounters.

In summary, a broker's pressure for commissions can work for you and against you. It's the old story: if it goes up, the broker earned his commission; but if it goes down, it was commission-motivated. If individuals were privy to the buying and selling constantly going on in trust departments, pension funds, and mutual funds, they might refer to that as "professional management," yet their record over the past five or six years is quite mediocre. True, some brokers wish to be the biggest producers rather than the best brokers; but in reality, the pressure to do the best for the customers supersedes everything. Besides, modern-day brokers have so many other areas of revenue that the everyday pressure on stock commissions is lessened. One-stop financial planning is becoming a reality. Your broker can now handle your stocks, bonds, mutual funds, annuities, various forms of insurance, tax-free municipal bonds, tax shelters, commodities, options, and—most recently—even home loans.

Schwartz: I was looking at my gains and losses for last year. I made $47,800, but I gave you commissions of $12,000.
Broker: That's only fair.
Schwartz: And what's my discount again?
Broker: 15%.
Schwartz: Why don't I declare you as a dependent?
Broker: Why don't I charge you by the hour? Then you'd owe me $25,000! If you paid an investment counselor 2% plus commissions, where would you be? With me, you get EST, TM, TA, politics, sports, the latest jokes, gossip, rumors, and all that good therapy.
Schwartz: Why don't you change your card to "Bon Vivant, Raconteur, and All-Around-Good-Guy"?
Broker: Seriously, we probably talk a total of two hours for every order written. Don't get me wrong, I'm well paid, but one of the reasons we are making money is because we talk things over a lot.

Schwartz: A broker is only as good as his last suggestion, and your last two are down five grand.

Broker: Only on paper, only on paper. You're starting to talk like a client again, and I have that strong suspicion we're about to talk about new issues.

Schwartz: How much Applicon am I getting?

Broker: 200 shares. The money you're making on new issues is paying for my commissions. You can tell everyone that your broker works for free.

Schwartz: 200 shares—that'll help the old net worth. As long as that goes up, I don't mind subsidizing you.

Broker: You know what Nelson Bunker Hunt said?

Schwartz: No.

Broker: Anyone who knows his net worth isn't worth much.

Schwartz: Give me a rundown, and I'll let you go back to flipping your account pages.

Broker: Well, the Dow has now climbed over 150 points and continues getting stronger. Everyone is looking the other way, concentrating on the election and the Republican convention.

Schwartz: I may be wrong, but I think the last time we had a presidential election *during a recession* was in 1960—Kennedy and Nixon. The market kept getting stronger toward election time and then took off the next year for 20 times earnings on the Dow by the end of '61.

Broker: And a Democrat got in who started acting like a Republican by cutting taxes and increasing depreciation allowances for business. Stock markets don't really care whether it's a Republican or Democrat as long as the economy moves without too much inflation.

Schwartz: You're right—my Open-Air says both parties

Broker:	are committed to that ... so how are your incoming calls now that we're up almost 150 points?
Broker:	Terrible. The Dow is flirting with 900, and a lot of people are still watching for that "next leg down."
Schwartz:	Good. When the inactives and the prospects and the "income" accounts start calling in with "What's hot?" let me know, and I'll start lightening up.
Broker:	You mean when I start drawing crowds at cocktail parties again, you're selling?
Schwartz:	No offense—it's Open-Air.
Broker:	Well, with respect to the market, we've got further to go because even with this volume, a lot of brokers are groaning over their gross.
Schwartz:	That's a case where brokers turn analyst, and it's their customers who suffer because they're not passing on their own firms' recommendations. Your firm's analysts are still bullish, aren't they?
Broker:	Our fundamentalists are bullish; research is bullish; but we have two technicians, and one is bullish and one is bearish. Both sides have to be heard.
Schwartz:	You know another reason this market's going into new high ground?
Broker:	Why?
Schwartz:	It's because everyone is surprised when they ask me, "How's the market?" and I say, "Great." When they're not aware of it and still out of it, then there's more room at the top.
Broker:	Have you seen what all these new issues are doing?
Schwartz:	Only the ones you got for me. I hear Anthem's gone from 13½ to 17, Cado Systems gone from

18 to 22, and Enzo Biochem's gone from 6¼ to 10.

Broker: Your Applicon came at 22 and it's now 32. Magnuson Computer came at 20 and it's now 25 ... and that's in a week!

Schwartz: I'm going to surprise you with a stock: Sears.

Broker: Sears? But those are declining earnings. It's the consumer getting caught in the squeeze between inflation and high energy costs. He's going to the discounter. Where's the Open-Air on this one?

Schwartz: True, and I'm probably early, but Sears is shaking up its management and turning things around. Besides I'm getting an insurance company with a retail operation thrown in. I've talked to several of their department managers and they're quite enthusiastic. Anyway I don't buy *all* Open-Air.

Broker: Schwartz, you're savvy enough to call your own shots, and you gave me $12,000 in commissions last year. Why don't you use a discounter?

Schwartz: Because I might save four grand in commissions and lose $20,000 a year in bad market moves. I'm smart enough to place high dollar value on feedback, research, and just plain talking things over.

Broker: You could ask for research reports from several brokerage firms and then place your order through a discounter.

Schwartz: That backfires! A few of my friends tried that, and they're out in left field if the brokerage firm changes its opinion about the market or a particular stock. Take the last market decline—your firm became bullish, you were pushing me, and as a result, we bought practically on the bottom. My friends are still on the sidelines.

Broker: Incidentally, Shearson is 41⅞, up from 27. Indiana, Ohio, and Juniper are all up. Oils are strong. That darn Minnetonka is now up another 3, and even Kodak is strong.

Schwartz: Look, do-it-yourselfers are penny-wise and pound-foolish. They will never make the big hit. I've got a chance dealing with you, and I don't at the discount house. I want you to call me with everything you hear or read. It's the constant input that helps me in my Open-Air Analysis. I place demands on you. I expect you to take advisory services and share the information with me. Again, it's not just information, but interpretation that I want.

Broker: Our best moves have been made in down markets. That's when you should be able to tell the difference between a broker and a salesman.

Schwartz: Listen, don't get carried away. I've told you—everyone should have a stockbroker! Our running dialogue helps my life. It keeps me up-to-date on interest rates, money markets, politics, and even the latest movies. My business and social life both prosper!

Broker: How about an order in return for all this BS?

Schwartz: Okay, buy 500 Sears.

Broker: Now I'm going to put you on to two Open-Air stocks: Stride Rite and Waste Management. Have you heard of the preppie look?

Schwartz: Hell, no.

Broker: Well, your Tony Lama boots are turning out to be a big money maker, and your Open-Air spotted that in the Western craze; now it's the preppie look. There's even a popular book on it.

Schwartz: What's Stride Rite got to do with the preppie look?

Broker:	They make Sperry Top Siders, the "in" shoe for college kids, executives. Man, you've got to have those Sperrys.
Schwartz:	Like Minnetonka and Softsoap—they can't keep them in stock?
Broker:	Right. The stock is 16. Had a down year last year, but now that shoe earnings are coming on strong, they could earn $1.80 in 1980 and maybe $2.20 in 1981.
Schwartz:	Let me check around some shoe stores. Now what about Waste Management?
Broker:	Ever looked at the name on the truck that picks up your garbage every week?
Schwartz:	Come on—you expect me to buy stock in garbage trucks?
Broker:	They're picking up a hell of a lot of waste disposal franchises in the country. Plus they dispose of nuclear material. Great growth record. It sells for 62 on about $3.50 earnings, but it's growing about 25–30% a year.
Schwartz:	Another one of those stocks selling for 15 times earnings, but growing at 25, thereby making it a buy?
Broker:	Now you're starting to get with it. Waste Management even landed the contract for the sanitation service of Riyadh, Saudi Arabia.
Schwartz:	Get me some stuff on these, but go ahead and buy 100 Waste Management, and let me study them.
Broker:	100 shares? Nothing like conviction.
Schwartz:	You've forgotten how many times I've started out this way and then kept buying. It's just that my Open-Air bell is not ringing.

7

THE CLIENT

"The best way to make money in the stock market is to buy good stocks and hold 'em til they go up and then sell 'em. If they don't go up, don't buy 'em."
—*Will Rogers*

What is a client? A broker's client is a human being in need of constant advice about money. Clients need advice on stocks, tax shelters, tax-free municipal bonds, corporate bonds, treasury bills, money markets for parking funds temporarily, options and commodities for speculating, and what to do for long-term safety and income.

The client is a multifaceted being, capable of reflecting the three emotions of investing:

Hope   Greed   Fear

We are all clients! The president of the United States is a client. The chairman of the Federal Reserve Board is a client of someone, and so is the president of General Motors, and your doctor; everybody is reacting to current events with one of the three emotions above. Do some of them have more inside information than others? Yes, but it's all relative. Since we are human, no matter what our station, we will always suspect someone else has the inside. In reality, our investing emotion goes something like the drawing on the following page.

A quick observation of this chart quickly reveals important conclusions about the emotions surrounding our in-

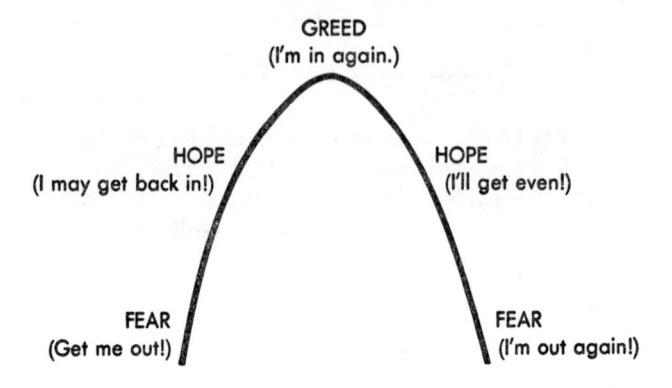

```
            GREED
         (I'm in again.)
            ╱‾‾╲
     HOPE  ╱    ╲  HOPE
(I may get╱      ╲(I'll get
  back in!)       even!)
         ╱        ╲
   FEAR ╱          ╲ FEAR
(Get me out!)    (I'm out again!)
```

vesting habits. Since most of us have little confidence of our own, we are largely influenced by the crowd: our peers, "they." If "they" are buying real estate, then why aren't we? If "they" are buying Mercedes, then why aren't we? If "they" start buying stocks, why don't we?

So, we enter the chart at the point of hope. Our stocks go up. (Our friends watch and, in turn, start the game at hope.) Then we hear stories that others might be making more money than we. Why aren't *we* in: Computervision, Lear Petroleum, Butte Gas and Oil, MA/COM or Teledyne? Then we move up the chart to greed! Greed stays around for a while. It's the "biggie" in our lives. An investor who starts off being greedy is okay. She, or he, exemplifies the following conversation:

"Good morning, I'd like to buy a stock."
"Fine. What kind of stock are you looking for?"
"The kind that goes up—what other kind is there?"

No communication problem here. She understood risk and clearly spelled out her objective: capital gains. Her broker was not forced into three or four months of experimenting with buys and sells before some emotional moment in the market brought her real objective to the surface.

The client who has not been honest about greed might have this conversation:

"Why are we in utilities when the market is booming? Look at the oils and technology stocks."

"But you said income and safety."

"Well, you're supposed to get me out of utilities and into growth on the way up and then back into utilities on the way down."

"You mean buy on greed and sell on fear."

A client can move around frequently, and it's called short-term trading or money management. If the broker moves around in the same fashion, it's called churning. Clients can create so many parameters for their brokers that they wind up getting mediocre advice. Brokers tend to migrate toward those clients who are secure in their objectives. This is comfortable and generally brings success, but it often takes time. The client who is only looking for the "kind that go up" is probably on the broker's first team even if he or she only has $10,000. First team members don't have conflicts about "dividends," "how long are we going to hold?" and "it's too risky," etc.

Some clients are thrill seekers; thrills are more important than making money, so they buy thrill stocks. Benny Buy Out is their broker. Action, action is a way of life:

Spreads, straddles, and puts and calls.
Drop shots, top spin lobs, fading left to right.
Exactas, daily doubles, pick-six.
Take the Yankees in six.
Yeah, yeah.

When the smoke clears, they break even at best. They get their thrills and the *broker* makes the money. One day a thrill seeker sent her broker a Christmas card with $100 in it. He called her and said, "Mrs. Seeker, the New York Stock Ex-

"When I refer to it as disposable income, don't get the wrong idea."

change Rules say I cannot accept anything over $25 and, besides, you paid me commissions; this is not necessary." Her reply to him was, "Well, I go over to Vegas and gamble, and I always tip the boys over there, so I don't know why I can't tip you." It takes all types!

SOME DO'S FOR CLIENTS ON THE WAY TO MAKING MONEY

PRACTICE DISCIPLINE

Probably the greatest obstacle to success in the stock market is the lack of discipline: hold winners and sell losers! We are all subject to gaining confidence solely through price action. We look at General Motors at 50. If it goes to 45 we forget it, but if it goes to 55, then we find courage to put in a limit order to buy at 50. "They," that mysterious unknown group who always are buying, have pushed it up so that the individual now gains confidence at 50.

OVERCOME GREED

Follow the rule of Confucius: when riding a tiger, it is best to have a plan for dismounting.

OVERCOME FEAR

Instead of taking the phone off the hook during bad markets, get your basket out and pick up the bargains as in October 1978, 1979, and March 1980.

BE PATIENT, NOT STUBBORN
(there's a difference)

Your stock hasn't done anything for two months. Having patience means if the fundamentals of your stock are still good, and the same reasons exist for owning it, then only two decisions are required:

>Buy more.
>Hold what you have.

But, if you refuse to accept a deteriorating picture like Itel or Chrysler in 1980, then you are *stubborn*. In one instance, a stock might be down or not performing because it is being overlooked by the market. In the other, red signals are clearly flashing.

PROFESSIONAL DISCIPLINES TO PRACTICE WITH YOUR BROKER

Once you have been baptized a "client," one who has experienced both profit and loss, there are some professional disciplines you can practice with your broker:

If you are getting prospect calls from strange brokers, you had best listen very carefully, because it's probably the bottom. After severe market drops, even veteran brokers are forced to place prospect calls. Immediately go back to your original broker and start the ball rolling. Interestingly enough, brokers get good ideas at bottoms, but are often discouraged by their own clients.

Watch for other signs, such as your broker pushing blue chips at bottoms and speculations at tops (it should be just the reverse). Take the long-term view if you want to make a lot of money. There is an old story of a client who took the long-term view for his kids and the short-term view for himself. After five years, his kids were worth more than he was.

Learn to take a loss. Stocks are like employees: some of them have to be fired because of poor performance.

Don't tell your broker you are out of money just to keep from hurting his feelings. If you don't like his recommendation, say so; but *don't* cause your broker to feel it's of no use to call: the next several calls might be quite profitable.

Don't become a market expert. We can lose out by always insisting, "I'll wait for the next leg down," or "It's going lower." A broker hates to be placed in the position of a salesman by a long-time, good client. As one stated: "I'm ready to fire a good account. We've been together for five years and have done very well, but lately (because he missed a big market move) he makes me feel like a door-to-door salesman with 'I don't like autos; I don't like drugs; oils are too high,' etc., etc."

When visiting your broker during market hours, don't be offended if she glances at a screen or accepts phone calls. She might have open orders for other clients near critical points and, after all, the phone is her livelihood. One broker told of a client/social friend who did very little business but invariably showed up during market hours to talk tennis!

Don't do business with close friends; both of you start pressing. Becoming casual friends with your broker is ideal, but close friends—no! It's the client who loses the most in these situations, because it's his money that goes if the broker loses objectivity. Friend or not, only do business with a broker who performs.

In one particular broker/client/friend relationship, the client had a hard time accepting his broker/friend's advice. You know how we all are with our close friends: somehow they just don't appear as professional to us as they do to other people. This broker solved the problem by becoming a "conduit." Everything became:

"My firm says..."

"*Wall Street Week* says..."

"Another broker in the office has this client who is president of..."

"*Forbes* recommends..."

Even when the ideas were his own, he employed the third-party pitch. Close friends of a broker need to remember that even though the broker is a commission salesman they can get the best out of him if the relationship is always one of discussion. Don't put yourself in the position of making him pitch while you choose and reject.

Don't second-guess your broker. But don't be afraid to ask him to go back over the reasons you bought or sold a stock. If you have hit two stocks in a row that have dropped a couple of points, and you start needling him, then you won't get the third suggestion. There is a difference between needling and honest questions, and the former may cause him to turn cautious on expressing how he really feels about the two you own, which are down.

Make every effort to stay in sync with each other. Here's how it works:

Broker tells you about Tom Brown, a young, domestic oil company, at 25 and you buy it. At 45, the broker recommends selling it and buying Bethlehem Steel. Bethlehem sits there for three months, and Tom Brown goes to 60.

You bring up the mistake (even though you could have gone back into Tom Brown) and say, "Find something that's moving, and let's get the hell out of Bethlehem." The broker doesn't want to buy into something that has already moved a lot, so he uncovers an overlooked stock like Goodyear. You get out of Bethlehem at 23 and into Goodyear at 16. Two months later Bethlehem is 28 and Goodyear is 16. Tom Brown is 70. "What's the quote on ol' man Brown?" You keep resurrecting the broker's mistake.

The broker now hears a story about Graphic Scanning at 24, but calls other clients instead of you. "Let Joe rest a while and make a profit on that position in Goodyear. All I need to do is get him out of Goodyear and have it go to 20, and I'll never hear the end of it," explains the broker. Then Graphic Scanning goes to 50 in three months, and you become a member of one broker's "Can't do anything right for Joe" club.

Seek out a winner for a broker—someone who thinks you can make a lot of money in the market; in fact, looks for it. Some brokers can't find a can of oil in a K Mart! In the midst of strong markets and new emerging growth companies, many brokers only see the "old favorites." Clients who are losers often end up with brokers who are losers. They buy Teledyne at 23 and sell it at 26, reflecting the real lack of long-term confidence needed to be a winner. Believe it or not, some clients don't want to make money. They only want to be right and be heroes. They look at the new low list instead of the new high list. It's called "bottom fishing," and their lines may be shorter than the real bottom.

In summary, clients improve their chances for making money by clearly stating objectives. The bottom line is either safety and income or growth. Of course, it varies, but the capital gains client who moans about no income when his stocks are down sets the stage for getting a much more conservative recommendation the next time. "If only clients knew," said one broker, "that the greatest pressure on a broker is for someone to say, 'You're the broker, tell me what to do.'" This gets the best out of the broker, and most clients search for someone to say that to.

Schwartz: Okay, let's have an understanding.
Broker: We work together.
Schwartz: That sounds good, but what it really means is that I take credit for the winners and blame you for the losers.
Broker: Fair enough for $12,000 gross.
Schwartz: Right! At cocktail parties I'll brag about the winners and call you a dummy for the losers.
Broker: Easy! You may talk yourself into no discounts.
Schwartz: And furthermore, I will never refer anyone to you because I want you all to myself.
Broker: I owe my soul to 100% Schwartz.
Schwartz: Now that we have that straight, let's make some money. Anything excite you?
Broker: I've got an Open-Air stock for you.
Schwartz: I'm listening.
Broker: Zenith. The stock is 14½ and just reported a second quarter that's almost doubled.
Schwartz: Who's buying TVs in a recession?
Broker: The TV is becoming as important as the toilet.

It's turning into a home information center, with cable TV, pay TV, over-the-air TV, and the biggest thing of all—video discs starting next year. The home computer will eventually hook up to the TV, and Zenith is in home computers by virtue of its purchase of Heath.

Schwartz: Toilet companies aren't exactly making new highs. What's the high and low, and what'll they earn this year?

Broker: It got down to 7⅞ on Bunker Hunt day, and the high is 13. They could earn $1.20 or $1.30 this year.

Schwartz: I hate paying 13 times earnings for a TV company. Is there a dividend?

Broker: I thought you didn't care about dividends. The dividend is 60¢, which is a 4½% yield, but look—they bought Heath from Schlumberger for cash, and those earnings are starting to come in now. Second, this puts them into the home computer market in about the $3,000 to $5,000 category. Next summer they will release video discs. That's a multibillion-dollar industry with not many players. You've got Zenith and RCA teamed up against MCA and North American Philips. In home computers, look what's happened to Tandy and Commodore International. They have both tripled. And don't forget what impact the offering on Apple Computer will have. It comes this fall.

Schwartz: Now you're getting to me! It's like the gambling stocks. There were only six or seven to own. The same with stock-brokerage companies.

Broker: Well, you made a ton on Rival Manufacturing after they introduced the Crock-Pot. This is more technical, but similar in that they are consumer-oriented. Right now, the home computer is being bought mostly by small businesses, but that market, plus the home market, is unlimited.

Schwartz: Didn't Zenith once sell in the 40s?

Broker: Actually, the all-time high was 85 but it sold at 40 back in 1976. Earnings were over $2.00, so it sold at 20 times earnings.

Schwartz: What's the book?

Broker: Book is around $15, and net working capital is around $13.

Schwartz: You don't find many technology stocks selling less than book. Have you contacted the company?

Broker: Yes, and they are sending you the 10-K and annual report, plus I've introduced myself to their financial PR.

Schwartz: What's the P/E on Motorola and RCA?

Broker: Ten times earnings. Actually, Zenith should have a higher P/E now with Heath, home computers, and videodiscs. If they could get those earnings back to $1.75-2.00 by the end of 1982, the stock could sell at 15 times earnings or 30.

Schwartz: What's the average P/E in the last five years?

Broker: Taking out the depressed year, it's about 12. Hell, Sony has sold as high as 30 times earnings and if you like Ford because of the "buy American" mood building up, then you ought to love this stock.

Schwartz: What's my buying power?

Broker: $42,000.

Schwartz: Okay, buy 1,000. Wait, what're the bid and asked, and the quote and size?

Broker: Come on, don't start that at your stage of the game. Losers place limit orders.

Schwartz: Go ahead, but I'll bet you lunch you get the high of the day.

Broker: Today's high might be tomorrow's low, and it won't be the first time. I'll bet you a lunch, with all the money you're making, that you can't name me the issues that we paid the high of the day for. In case you're interested, you paid the high of the day for Tony Lama, Sensormatic, Ohio, and Minnetonka. What if limit orders had caused you to miss them?

Schwartz: While we're talking it's probably up another ¼. You're costing me money already.

Broker: Done.

⟨ 8 ⟩

STOCK MARKET WINNERS OR LOSERS TEST

(MAYBE YOU SHOULD STAY IN A PASSBOOK SAVINGS ACCOUNT)

The best investor is the one who has made the most mistakes.

STOCK MARKET EXAM 101

Do you:

1. Buy on the high of the day and sell on the low?
2. Always hear about something after it has doubled?
3. Get into the market just before a major correction?
4. Sell a stock that goes up while simultaneously buying one that goes down?
5. Stay in a stock for six months while it does nothing; get out and have it double?
6. All of the above?

PERSONALITIES OF WINNERS AND LOSERS

It's been said that the price you pay for being an investor isn't worth the price you get. For some people that is true: we call them losers. Others, who have experienced the learning curves of investing and profited by them, are called winners.

The personality trait of Louie Loser and his corresponding market actions are outlined as follows:

PERSONALITY TRAIT	MARKET ACTION
Greed, but no self-confidence.	Must gain confidence through price action. Looks at Butte Gas & Oil at 16, 18, and 20, then places a limit order at 16.
Can't take a loss. It's another way of saying he can't make it up.	Follows stock down from 25 (greed), to 23 (hope), to 19 (fear), and finally blows it out in a moment of emotion at 15; the emotion of a piece of news (Reagan's rumored heart attack and a 22-point drop), crossed with existing fear produces—panic!

Example:

"But I don't want to take that loss."

"The fundamentals are deteriorating, Louie. Their sales and earnings have collapsed, and IBM has announced a better product."

"It'll come back."

"What's your portfolio worth?"

"$85,000—down from $100,000 three months ago."

"But up from $70,000 at the end of the year. And we have not added any money."

"What's your point?"

"If you sell $10,000 worth of a bad one, then what is your portfolio worth?"

"$85,000. But the next stock might be worse."

"Louie, we're just bringing in another pitcher! All the other team members stay in their same positions, but this one member of the portfolio is getting bombed."

"What about buying more?"

"You know our discipline. If the fundamentals are the same and nothing has changed except the market, then look at buying more. But this is different. Sales and earnings both are down, and a big competitor is killing us. Louie, stocks are like employees: most of them keep working for you even though they have their slumps, but when an employee stops working and productivity falls, get rid of him."

"Let's watch it." (Which means avoid decision.)

PERSONALITY TRAIT	MARKET ACTION
Peter Peer Group, can't stand it because he thinks everyone else is doing better.	Doesn't hold positions, jumps around, and has done business with eighteen brokers (none good).

Example:

"Peter, how may I help you?"

"I'm only interested in income, and I can't take any risks. The money I have is really only my money for six months; then it must be distributed among my family."

"Is this a trust?"

"No, but we have to keep it in my name with my brother."

"A joint account?"

"Right, and we can't speculate on anything—just something that's safe."

"Well, you'd better put it in a money market fund or T-bills."

"Uh . . . well, not that conservative. Haven't you got something that pays a good dividend and might be up a little in six months?"

"It might also be down. You placed a time limit of six months."

"Oh, I know, but, yes, we've got to beat inflation."

"Peter, a conservative portfolio could be a couple of utilities, Exxon, GM, and Colgate."

"Okay."

Two months later:

"Why didn't you put me in Computervision or Datapoint or Tandy?"

"You wanted no risk."

"But I didn't say I wanted very little performance. My friends are getting rich."

"Peter, you said the money had to be in place within six months. Stock markets are seldom accommodating. Hell, we could be in a Mideast war. Trying to be conservative with some risk in a six-month time frame is not fair to your money. But if you want me to guess with your money, I'll go ahead."

"We've got four months left. Let's get some of these things that are moving. Just do it, I'll be responsible."

Three months later (and a market correction of 80 points):

"Damn, we've bought and sold, and the only

one who's made out is you. I'm down ten grand; what do I say to my brother?"

"Tell him your broker made you do it!"

PERSONALITY TRAIT	MARKET ACTION
Invests based on *today's* headlines. Needs written verification by someone else.	Gets in at tops and out at bottoms. Consistent losers base their decisions on today's headlines. By the time a stock or a stock market reaches a headline category, most of the move is over.

Example:

Take the case of Harriet Headline in February 1980. Silver was making headlines at $50 an ounce before it plunged to $13:

"Get me out of my stocks, and let's buy silver. No one owns stocks anymore and no one has dollars. The world has changed."

"Harriet, just because we're having a market correction doesn't mean the world is coming to an end."

"Are you kidding? Back in November '79 *Business Week* said equities were dead!"

"Look, it's February 1980, an election year. Several bids are before Congress to lower capital gains tax and eliminate double taxation. The re-industrialization of the U.S. is becoming a buzz word. That means tax breaks for business. Regardless of who gets elected, the eighties could be great for the stock market."

"Don't you read the headlines? Everyone is converting cash and stocks into gold, silver, antiques, and real estate. Go ahead and cash me out and use the money to buy two contracts of silver."

One month later, plus eighteen straight days when silver was down the limit (you can't get out when a commodity is down the limit):

"This Bunker Hunt fiasco has wiped me out, plus I owe your firm another $35,000. What do I tell my husband and children?"

"Tell them your broker made you do it!"

PERSONALITY TRAIT	MARKET ACTION
Impatient, needs action in his stock in order to confirm faith in himself. Is only satisfied by the everyday *action* of his stocks, not the long-range performance.	A trader. Goes from options to commodities, trying to get new issues. Must make a *little* money fast. Can't make a *lot* of money slow. Alan Action strikes again!

Example:

"I've tried this stock market, and it's no good. Hell, you can't beat the institutions. But I've got a terrific deal if you want to go in with me."

"What's that?"

"Skateboard parks! And racquetball courts! Go ahead and sell my MA/COM, Amerada Hess, and Zenith, and send me a check."

Two months later: the obvious. Alan was the last one in the chain letter. The fad was over—skateboard parks were being plowed under, and MA/COM, Amerada Hess, and Zenith doubled.

PERSONALITY TRAIT	MARKET ACTION
Appreciates a winner whether it's a theater performance, a horse, a great person, a stock, or a sports team. Seldom roots for the underdog: bets on emerging new champions, like Spectacular Bid, Tom Watson, and John McEnroe, or existing winners like Bill Shoemaker.	Is attracted by success; doesn't disbelieve it. At the proper time, is found in energy stocks, computer stocks, health care, stock-brokerage stocks, etc. Is generally early and has confidence in her own judgment.

Example, Wilma the Winner:

"I'm probably early, but I think I'll start buying companies involved in the mobile phone business. Who's in the industry?"

"If you mean the cellular phones or radio paging, Wilma, there's Graphic Scanning at 20, E & F Johnson at 11, Radiofone at 8, Motorola at 48, and American Telephone at 51. This is a biggie, because the cellular approach to communications permits virtually unlimited telephone use in vehicles. But nothing can happen until the FCC gives approval. That could be another year."

"I said I was early, and I don't mind waiting in order to be in at the ground level. The eighties will be the decade of the mobile telephone."

"AT&T has the patents, and mobile phones will probably be leased, not sold, so with the deregulation of communications continuing, I believe all companies will have a crack at this."

"I only bet on the leader, the champion. Who would that be? If not the champion, then the emerging champion?"

"Never mind what I look like—I want something risky."

"Graphic Scanning has the largest stake in radio paging, so should profit the most; although E & F Johnson is a pure play. To tell you the truth, Wilma, you can spread your bets at this stage and after the race has been run for a while, you will be able to see who's in front."

"Okay. Get me 300 Graphic, 500 E & F Johnson, 500 Radiofone, and 200 Motorola. Get 100 American Telephone: mobile phones might finally do it for them."

WHAT ARE SOME OTHER CHARACTERISTICS OF WINNERS AND LOSERS?

Let's take a test to find out where you stand:

1. When you have made up your mind about a stock, do you

a. Buy the stock, or its underlying option?
b. Place a market or a limit order?
c. Place a stop-loss order immediately upon purchase?

Answer a: winners buy stocks, losers buy the option. It is an accepted fact that 80% of option traders who buy puts or calls lose money.

Answer b: winners buy at the market, losers place limit orders. A limit order is an expression of no confidence.

Answer c: placing stop-loss orders at the time of purchase is another way of saying "I don't know what I'm doing."

2. Do you buy low-priced or high-priced stocks?

Winners do both, but probably spend more time in stocks above 20. Losers are attracted to low price. In a winner's portfolio you will find both. In a loser's, you will find mostly low prices.

3. How many stocks do you own that are going to be "bought out"?

Winners look for fundamentals, losers must have the crutch of a "buy-out."

4. Do you only buy stocks whose earnings and dividends are increasing *now*?

Many stocks have their biggest moves in *anticipation* of big earnings and subsequent dividend increases. On the way up in dramatic fashion, they often sell at 20 to 30 times earnings and then flatten out when the earnings start arriving. Losers are addicted to the present or past and must have immediate visibility to earnings. Losers have a hard time buying a stock for 20-plus times earnings because this forces them to forecast several years in advance.

5. Which emotion causes you the most mistakes: greed or fear?

Winners might become overextended or too heavily concentrated in one issue, but they are not frightened out of the game. To win, you must stay in the game. Losers pick up their marbles and go home—generally at the bottom. A winner generally errs on greed; a loser errs on fear.

6. Which influences your investment decision the most?
   a. The condition of the market?
   b. The condition of the company?

Winners pick stocks, losers watch the market.

7. Which investment experience might fit your background?
   a. Twelve trades a year with 8 gains, 4 losses. Net result: loss.
   b. Twelve trades a year with 4 gains, 8 losses. Net result: gain.

A winner looks at his confirms at tax time and has succeeded in having small losses and large gains. Even if it were a difficult year in the market, producing more losses, they were kept small and didn't overcome the few big winners. It's generally the stocks that are *held* in the portfolio that do the job. Winners can go long-term, losers can't.

8. The most money you have ever made has been in
   a. Bull markets.

15. When you buy a stock, which of the following most closely reflects your initial thoughts?
    a. "If it doesn't move, I'll kick it out."
    b. "I'll take the 3 or 4 points and run."
    c. "The stock is 20 and should sell for 40."

Only a fool buys anything that will give him a small return. When a broker and client can't justify a large gain in a stock over a year or two, then go to another one.

16. Which has been the toughest for you?
    a. Making money in the market.
    b. Keeping the money you have made.

You're not a winner unless you keep it. Cashing out along the way and getting tax-free bonds or other areas of diversification is just plain good financial planning.

17. When do you find yourself the most active in the market?
    a. When the volume is 70 million shares.
    b. When the volume is 40 million shares.

The higher the volume, the closer the top or bottom. After major market breaks like March 1980, it often happens that stock markets start *up* on low volume, like a train whose big wheels start turning slowly as it begins to leave the station. High volume is another example of Harriet Headline. In August 1980, after a 200-point advance had already taken place, Merrill Lynch said, "Buy aggressively." Many advisory services then started turning bullish while the market had only another 70 points to go. Near that top of 1,000, the high volume (80 million shares) and bullish headlines were attracting investors like Harriet Headline. During the week that the market hit 1,000, the stock market appeared on the cover of *Newsweek*. Three weeks later, it had dropped 100 points. Typically, after a 200-point drop and when the volume dries up to 40 million shares or so, winners start placing their bets.

18. Which comes easiest for you?
    a. Buying on good news.
    b. Buying on bad news.

It depends on the bad news. You could have started buying Chrysler at 20 on its first bad news and ridden it down to 6. As a rule of thumb, the good news had probably already been discounted. Perhaps a better approach is to buy on the *first* piece of good news after a series of bad news releases. Zenith's stock, after falling for four years from 40 to 10 with a series of bad earnings reports and losses of market share to the Japanese, suddenly had two successive good earnings reports—the second coming with the stock at 12. Within six months the stock had moved to 21.

19. Once you have sold a stock at a loss, which comes easiest?
    a. Looking for another company as a replacement.
    b. Considering where to buy back stock you just sold.

Once you have had a loser, don't have a reconciliation! If you get back into the same stock, you demand even more of it the second time, and you don't think as well with the memory of a previous loss. Look for a new stock—there are roughly 60,000 of them.

20. A middle-management person is telling you how great his company is. Your broker doesn't follow the company, but sends you the latest information, together with a generalized opinion. Your next step is to
   a. Watch the stock for a few days.
   b. Check with another broker.
   c. Get your broker to call the company or its competitors.

Naturally, you'll start watching the stock, but here's where winners and losers separate. Losers only watch the price action. Winners start researching the company, its competitors, its dealers, and also charting the stock.

21. A good story comes on a company and you have no spare cash. You plan to raise money from existing positions. Your first thought is to sell
   a. Stocks with profits.
   b. Stocks with losses.
   c. Stocks that haven't done anything.

If you never learn anything else, learn to sell losers, keep winners.

22. True or false: being bullish is generally more profitable than being bearish.

True. It doesn't mean being a Pollyanna, like the eternal optimist child, who, when dumped in a room with nothing but horse manure up to his knees, began to dig feverishly. "Why are you digging?" he was asked. "Must be a pony in here somewhere." A corny story, but descriptive of a stock market winner—always digging. It's just that much *more* profitable to look for opportunities in a horrible climate.

23. A strong market has been in force for several months and you're a "sold-out bull" sitting on the sidelines waiting for the next correction. The best thing to do is
   a. Go back into previous leaders even though you never owned them.
   b. Go back into stock on which you have previously made money.

   Go back into what you did best. Always get back on your winners. You know the stock: that's always a prerequisite to success.

24. A market decline has resulted in your equity falling to about 35% in your margin account. The best thing to do is
   a. Wait for the margin call.
   b. Sell before they tell you to sell.

   Investing is like fishing: you've got to have bait. Always keep your bait, so sell before they tell you to sell. Otherwise you might lose your line, pole, and fishing spot. And sell the weak ones.

25. When you begin receiving prospecting calls from other brokers, and your own broker is working later or on Saturdays, and this is combined with low volume and reports of brokerage-house mergers and pessimism, do you become
   a. Bullish?
   b. Bearish?

   It pays to start getting bullish in the midst of signals like these.

26. You buy a stock at 30, and it promptly goes to 35; or, conversely, it promptly goes to 25. Under which condition do you find yourself reviewing the reasons you bought the stock?
   a. When the stock goes to 35.
   b. When the stock goes to 25.

You constantly review when it goes up or down. The loser relaxes just because it's up; the winner constantly monitors.

In summary, if you can't afford to lose, you can't afford to win.

Broker: Well, Schwartz, 1980 is eight months old and a week ago Friday, the August 18 money supply figures were a disaster—the worst I've seen. Up $9 billion each on M1-A and M1-B.

Schwartz: I understand some of that is social security float, but how much is difficult to tell. What do you think?

Broker: Might be the excuse for that overdue correction.

Schwartz: Let's get our basket and put some "buys" in under the market. What's my buying power?

Broker: $40,000.

Schwartz: Okay, let's buy 300 more of Applicon at 32, making it 500; 400 Juniper at 17, making it 1,000; and 500 MCI Communications at 10, making it 1,500.

Broker: You're not one to use limit orders, 100%, why this time?

Schwartz: Only because I think it will be a short-lived correction, and I want to take my own emotion out of it.

Broker: Well, let's follow the one-eighth rule. Instead of 32 and 17 and 10, let's make it 32⅛, 17⅛, and 10⅛. Otherwise, it could drop back, hit round figures like those, and you'll be in competition with everyone else at the same prices: it's called "stock ahead."

Schwartz: Okay, do it! ... Incidentally, how much oil does Iraq export?

Broker: Iraq exports 3½ million barrels a day. One and a half through the Persian Gulf and two million through that aperture to the Mediterranean that was just blown up.

Schwartz: Which leaves how much world oil supply now?

Broker: They say about one hundred days of oil above the ground. So we now have climbing interest rates, a fear of an oil shortage, the Iraq/Iran war, and they raised the discount rate to 13%.

Schwartz: Open-Air Analysis says, "Why then are we not seeing gas lines like before?" Anyway, what's the market?

Broker: Down 15, but that isn't all—after the close on Friday, the money supply was up another two billion. Your MA/COM split, so that's good news.

Schwartz: How far down have we come?

Broker: Over 50 points. We were up to 968.

Schwartz: Is it time to be circling the wagons?

Broker: I don't think so. The Iraq/Iran deal is really a split-up of OPEC, and Saudi Arabia said it would increase production to 9½ million barrels a day. As for interest rates—we've seen them higher than this.

Schwartz: I should have known when *Investors Intelligence* showed 53.8% of the investment advisory services bullish vs. 20.4% bearish, and the previous week it was 40.2% bullish and 38% bearish.

Broker: And we are heading into our favorite month—October!
Schwartz: What's the latest T-bill auction?
Broker: 11.13%. We think this might be an interest rate blow off. 14 or 15% could be the peak.
Schwartz: Let's see how 900 or 910 in the averages holds. P/E ratios are getting out of line. IBM is 10 times earnings and Computervision is 30 times.
Broker: But Computervision is growing three times faster. It's simple: a company growing 20% a year but selling at 10 times earnings is still cheap.
Schwartz: And a company growing at 10% a year and selling for 20 times earnings is a sell candidate.
Broker: Right.
Schwartz: Back to the market. The election is only three weeks away. What's the feeling?
Broker: A toss-up. I went to a fancy meeting of economists yesterday and came away a little bearish.
Schwartz: No matter who is elected?
Broker: Right. Volcker still can't get a handle on the money supply, and we could have a November massacre—another round of tight money and higher interest rates.
Schwartz: Want a crash scenario? Have Volcker raise Fed funds and the discount rate on a Thursday, and then on a Saturday have Iran close the Strait of Hormuz.
Broker: And on the following Monday we're down 50 points. Forget the doom and gloom—what did you think of the Genentech offering?
Schwartz: How much did I get?
Broker: Not a whiff. Our entire office got 25 shares. In fact, 500 Merrill Lynch offices didn't get any, and no office got over 100 shares.

Schwartz: What did it do?
Broker: Came at 35, and the first price in the aftermarket was 80. It traded up to 89 bid and closed at 71¼.
Schwartz: So Robert Swanson, President of Genentech at thirty-two, holds 985,000 shares, making him worth about $75 million.
Broker: It's all in his genes.
Schwartz: What happened today?
Broker: Well, we were up 9 but finished down 13 on 65 million. Henry Kaufman did his thing.
Schwartz: I heard. Higher interest rates for the foreseeable future.
Broker: You have to respect him . . . he's called this interest-rate disaster on the nose. But I've got good news. Minnetonka split its stock again and reported big earnings. That Softsoap is humming. How long are you going to hold?
Schwartz: As long as my Open-Air field trips say to hold this stock. I have three stores where I always ask about Softsoap, and it's still selling like crazy. When one or two of them says it's slowing down—I'm gone! You know, I've made a ton on that stock already, and it was so obvious. Incidentally, what's Cooper Tire and Rubber?
Broker: 11. What's Open-Air about Cooper Tire and Rubber?
Schwartz: People are keeping their cars longer and therefore needing more replacement tires. Cooper is one of the biggest in that area.
Broker: Well, hold on, let me go get the Value Line and Standard & Poor's. . . . Okay, earnings were down for six months; book value is 26; half their sales are private labels; return on equity has fallen four years in a row; stock is thin, and some 32%

	is held by their own profit-sharing plan. I'm underwhelmed!
Schwartz:	Well, my gas station attendant says his replacement-tire business has really taken off in the last two months. I've checked Sears and Wards, and they say the same thing. What's the low on Cooper?
Broker:	9⅝.
Schwartz:	Hell, I can't go back on my Open-Air now, with the stock only 1⅜ off the low. Buy 500. If they suddenly get a good quarter, it could cut loose, it's so thin.
Broker:	Done.

WHEN TO FIRE YOUR BROKER

How have you done with your present broker? How have you done on your own? One way of evaluating a broker's performance is to match it against the pros and also against other leading averages.

The following represents the compounded annual rates of return for the five years ended December 30, 1979.* These are *total return* figures, which include capital gains and dividends.

Standard & Poor's 500	+14.7%
Dow Jones Averages	+12.0%
Salomon Brothers High-Grade Bond Index	+5.8%
Pooled equity funds of bank and insurance companies	+12.7%

Some quick conclusions on this are obvious. The pros, or big institutional money managers, did not even keep up with the Standard & Poor's and barely edged the Dow Jones Averages (+12.7% vs. 12%). Anyone taking refuge in the

---

* Source: Bernstein-Macaulay, Inc.

bond market for those old "safe harbor" reasons of safety and income got killed. And yet, inflation was roaring ahead at an average of 13%, so where were the heroes?

Should a broker or investment advisor who can't beat the averages be fired? *Yes!*

The main reason for switching brokers is simple: your broker is not making enough money for you. It might even be your fault, but if you have given the broker at least a year and have taken all of his advice and still come up short, then get a "divorce."

In fairness to yourself and the broker, be sure you are measuring portfolio performance correctly. For instance, one broker reports a client (divorced and needing income) made eight trades in two years, all at profits. She transferred her account because at *one* point in time, "It wasn't doing anything." On further examination of that *one* point in time, her portfolio went into the March 1980 180-point slide worth $74,000 and came out of it in June worth $76,000. The broker made no panicky suggestions and merely rode it through, but the client misinterpreted the inactivity as "going nowhere." It's funny how *income* clients get dissatisfied with no performance.

Some brokers, and it is often found in young brokers, can become almost kamikaze in their approach to clients' money. Wild trading, particularly in options, becomes a form of self-destruction. The new broker is not thinking about building long-term capital, but instead is concentrating on near-term commissions.

HOW TO TELL THE DIFFERENCE BETWEEN A BROKER AND A SALESMAN

A *broker* says "I" when the stock he recommends is either up or down. A *salesman* says "I" when it's up and "we" when it's down. It is said that clients take credit for the ones that are up and blame the broker for the ones that are down, but *salesmen* have the following traits:

> They recommend so many issues so often that they forget their pitch.
> They sell you what is easy and generally at the top: gambling stocks, computer leasing, oil services.

Brokers believe in their recommendations enough to advise when you should average down. Salesmen say, "Get out." Brokers will admit to a mistake; salesmen ignore it. Brokers will reveal what they are doing in their own account; salesmen, for the most part, don't have their own money in the market. A salesman might look good temporarily in a bull market, but a broker performs in bull *and* bear markets.

Don't confuse brains with a bull market.

HOW TO TELL IF YOU HAVE THE WRONG BROKER

Do you feel you can't call him or her at any time for advice unless "the meter is running"? If you have an idea on a particular stock, does your broker take your order with an "it's your funeral" attitude? At the end of the year when you add up all of your transactions, has the broker made more money than you? This could happen occasionally, but don't make a career out of it. You should fire the salesman and keep the broker!

HOW DO YOU MEASURE A BROKER?

Today, most brokerage firms provide monthly statements, which also serve as a mini portfolio review. This is only for street name accounts, which will be discussed in greater detail in the chapter entitled "Tips on Managing Your Portfolio." Suffice it to say, it is much easier to measure yourself, and your broker, if your securities are in street names. At the end of every month, your statement tells you where you are.

At any rate, take your statements ending December of each year and compare the portfolio market values. Next, add to that figure all of the dividends you have received for the year. Add or subtract monies taken out of or put into the account. Finally, divide the difference by the ending portfolio value. For example:

December 30, 1979, statement of market value	$78,000
December 30, 1980, statement of market value	91,000
December 30, 1980, statement of year-end total dividends	4,680
Money taken out in March, August, and October—not dividends, but sale of stock for personal use	8,000
Money added in February statement	4,000

So, in figuring how well you have done, take

December 30, 1980, market value	$91,000
Plus total dividends received	+ 4,680
	$95,680
December 30, 1979, market value	$78,000
Plus money added in February	+ 4,000
Minus money taken out for personal use	− 8,000
	$74,000

Total ending gain in portfolio for year (plus dividends)	$95,680
Minus total beginning portfolio value plus or minus monies added	74,000
Net gain	$21,680
Percent gain for year* (21,680 ÷ 74,000)	+29%

If the Dow Jones was up that year 20% and the Standard & Poor's was up 25%, you have indeed outperformed both market averages.

What if your broker is performing well, but his firm's statements are wrong and dividends get fouled up? A word to the wise on this: be on good terms with your broker's secretary; she will put out a lot of fires for you. Seven out of ten calls she answers are complaints, so courtesy and friendliness will help get the job done.

TIPS ON GETTING THE BEST FROM YOUR BROKER

Wall Street reacts, it does not create. In March 1980 Wall Street reflected the gold and silver greed of certain individuals; this greed eventually led to a crash. Wall Street itself did not try to corner the market. But since it is made up of humans reacting to events, all too often Wall Street packages fads for sale to the public—at tops:

The REITs of the early seventies
The mutual funds of the late sixties

---

* If you have margin account interest, this is deductible.

The bond funds of the late seventies
The gold funds of the late seventies

And because of this, remember an old brokerage adage: "Whatever is toughest for the broker to sell his client is probably best for him or her. Whatever is easiest to sell is probably at the top."

So, if communication, computer, oil, or nursing-home stocks have been making new highs for over a year, it is likely the public starts to hear about it. If the broker at this point is trying to steer you into foods, drugs, or airlines—something that hasn't already doubled or tripled—but you would rather be "where the action is," then you make it *easy* for him to sell you what is popular, what is moving, and what is probably topping out. As pointed out earlier, once a group gets into gear, like the oils, it's a question of how far they have come. Don't be an easy sell just because something is popular. You might catch Auto-Train at 30 in 1978 on its way to 4 in 1980. Auto-Train captured the fancy of investors as an energy solution. If you wanted to go to Florida and see Disney World, you parked your car on a train in Washington, D.C., and rode down. More on this type of stock in chapter eleven.

Keep a diary next to the phone, not necessarily to trick your own broker, but to list facts and figures so that you can both go over them the next time. Most good brokers keep an extra piece of paper over your holding page to list stocks that you have talked about. You do the same! Watch out that it doesn't degenerate into an "I told you so" list. It can be very helpful going back and recalling when you discussed a certain stock and at what price. Remember, it's your money.

Also on this page you can note whenever he mentions that he bought something in his own account. Ask him how many shares. Three months later, if he originally said he bought 200 Amerada Hess in his own account at 28, you can ask him if he still has it. As a general rule, brokers will trade in their own account much more often than they will trade their clients' accounts. So, if your broker has sold his Amerada Hess in order to buy something else, but has kept all his clients in Amerada, that is quite typical. But if he divulges his positions, then you have a right to ask questions. Again, it's that team arrangement which is the winner.

Above all, don't make him feel like a salesman. The following conversation between Danny Decision and his broker might have taken place in the shoe department of Bloomingdale's:

"How's my magician?"

"Your magician?"

"Yeah, you're the only person I know who has a formula for making money disappear."

"Don't become Frankie Fairweather on me. So we're taking gas now, but this is the time to start buying."

"Like what?"

"We've come out with a recommendation on U.S. Home and..."

"I don't like home builders. What else?"

"American Brands has raised the dividend eight times in two years and has dropped to where it is yielding over 8% and..."

"I quit smoking. And besides, I don't like $60 stocks. Haven't you got something below 10?"

"House of Fabrics is an interesting spec at 4. In a recession we all turn to doing it ourselves and..."

"Nobody sews anymore. Come on, with all that research and advertising you ought to have something."

"Well, do you want my third, fourth, or fifth choices or my number one?"

"Soar like an eagle, my boy. Think independent—give me your best shot."

"How can I soar like an eagle when I'm dealing with turkeys?"

This client couldn't follow the rule of firing salesmen and keeping brokers. He would *always* have a salesman for a broker . . . he didn't know how to develop any other kind. When questioned on the subject, he was proud of two things:

> He had never made any money in the market.
> Brokers were all tipsters and he had fired fourteen of them in his career.

The unpardonable sin of a stockbroker is to become paralyzed in very weak markets. Whether a broker or his firm is right or wrong, clients deserve opinions in falling markets—while they are falling and recovering.

Paul Paralysis was a good broker, had a good clientele, and was an independent thinker. He was not a robot for his firm, but always represented its thinking as well as his own . . . until March 1980.

In his own mind he was right. The big one was here—1929 all over again, and the best thing he could do was get everyone out and into T-bills. His firm was advising playing it cool. Be like the jackrabbit; lie low and let the hailstorm blow. Paul did not even consider compromising his own feelings with those of his firm. Maybe tell his clients how he felt and also how the firm felt and be safe, and just sell 20 or 30%. No, it was everyone out of the pool. For a while, Paul was a hero . . . and then came the beginning of one of the sharpest rallies on Wall Street.

Climbing a "wall of worry," the Dow went up 225 points in the next five months. Almost all indicators moved to new high ground, and Paul's firm had been screaming "buy" almost from the bottom.

Paul had disbelieved. Paul was out of business! No one questioned his integrity, but a lot of clients were deprived of two things: having their own portfolios rebound, even if they bought nothing at the bottom, or making new purchases at bargain levels to improve their net worth.

If your broker is trying to get you into the market after a severe decline and you say no, that's your own error. But if your broker gets you out and never says when to get back in, or, worse yet, says nothing on the way down or up, he should be fired. The one exception to this would be if you are an older person with a portfolio of very conservative issues. Then perhaps the best strategy might be to "do nothing." Involving older people in emotional buying and selling is not justified.

It's always easy to look back: "If I," "would of," "could of," "should have," "ought to" are great 20-20 expressions. We will continue to have our share of scary moments in the market. When we do, turn to this chapter.

Listed below are just a few examples from a period when the New York Stock Exchange was having a "spring sale" in 1980. "Buy low and sell high," say the spectators and armchair quarterbacks. . . .

These prices start as of April 30, 1980, which is *one month* after the bloody unrealistic bottom set on March 27, Silver Thursday or Bunker Hunt day. Since a bottom is an area and not a point, and no one ever buys right *on* the bottom, let's just take the recovery from April 30 to August 30: four months!

	PRICE AT 4/30/80	PRICE AT 8/30/80
Aydin Corporation	17½	30½
Alcan Aluminum	25	31¾
Amerada Hess	23½	31
American Brands	65⅝	81
American Medical International	35⅛	46½
Ampex	19	24⅝
Atwood Oceanics	28½	46

	PRICE AT 4/30/80	PRICE AT 8/30/80
Auto-trol Technology	29¼	57
Bausch & Lomb	44	55¾
Bache	8⅜	14
Baker International	29½	35
Barry Wright	25	37½
Belco Petroleum	36¾	47
Beverly Enterprises	9⅜	17⅞
Bow Valley Industries	12	19½
Buttes Gas and Oil	12¾	25
Cabot Corporation	60⅝	85½
Campbell Red Lake	30½	59
Cenco	5¾	8⅛
City Investing	18⅝	26½
Commodore International	34	68
Computervision	22⅝	46
Control Data	52	71
Datapoint	50¼	74¼
Dean Witter Reynolds	13	22½
Denelcor	4	9¾
Dome Mines	61½	112
Eastman Kodak	52½	64
Esterline Corporation	26¼	49⅞
Exxon	60	70
Florida Steel	21½	34
Flow General	18	31¾
Fluke (John)	21¾	29
Freeport Minerals	26½	56
GCA	33¾	63
Geosource	58¼	83
Gerber Scientific	25	40½
Gillette	24⅝	30
Global Marine	25½	45¾
Goodyear	12¼	15¾

	PRICE AT 4/30/80	PRICE AT 8/30/80
Hospital Corporation of America	33¼	45⅞
Hughes Tool	57⅜	68½
Humana	40⅜	53
Hutton, E. F.	18¾	36¼
Intel	61⅜	87½
Intermark	10	18⅝
Jim Walter	27¾	34⅝
Kirby Explorations	63½	137
Lennar	18⅞	29¼
Lifemark	19¾	30½
Logicon	17	24
MA/COM	22¼	42
Magma Power	22⅞	28
Mary Kay	33¾	55½
Mattel	7¼	12½
MCI Communications	5⅞	9½
Merrill Lynch	19	30¼
Mesa Petroleum	28⅝	54¼
Mohawk Data Science	14½	26¾
Mitchell Energy & Development	24⅞	38
National Medical Enterprises	31⅜	43¼
Nicolet Instruments	15⅝	25¾
Nucor	41	55¾
Oak Industries	27⅛	37
Pacific Scientific	15½	34⅝
Palm Beach	13¾	19⅞
Paradyne	23½	39
Petro-Lewis	18⅜	28
Prime Computer	18	36¾
Reading & Bates	39¼	54

	PRICE AT 4/30/80	PRICE AT 8/30/80
Recognition Equipment	7⅛	15½
Rolm	19¾	36
Santa Fe International	33½	53
Scientific Atlanta	22	38½
Shearson Loeb Rhoades	17⅜	29⅜
Tandy	31¾	70
Teledyne	95⅜	165
Texas International Oil	19½	27
TIE Communications	7	14¼
Tom Brown	14½	25½
Topaz	14½	22
Towner Petroleum	15¼	27¾
Upjohn	51	57¾
Valtec (now a division of MA/COM)	18¾	40
Veeco Instruments	18	36⅞
Waste Management	44	70
Wainoco Oil	25⅜	36¾
Western Company of North America	47	68
Zenith	9⅞	16

in four months!

Did your broker try to make you do it? Maybe he tried and *you* failed, or you told him you were out of money or out of the market. But if you've had an active, continuing broker-client relationship, and he did not call and at least try to "make you do it," then fire him.

In summary, having the right broker is critical. It's the difference between success, mediocrity, or failure. There may be a breaking-in period, but once you both get into an Open-

Air groove, you should make money. You and your broker generally learn a lot about each other when taking losses. You may not like him, but if he is good and makes you money, stay with a good thing. Conversely, you may like him a lot, but no performance. Fire him!

10

WHEN A CLIENT MAY BE FIRED

"My statement is screwed up beyond all recognition!"
screamed Neal No-Business.

Neal has a $100,000 account in street name with special orders to mail his dividends to his bank once a month. In addition, he has instructed the brokerage firm to round out all rights offerings, and he gets automatic portfolio reviews every three months. He visits his broker during market hours to discuss his social life and tennis games and walks out with quotes and armloads of Standard & Poor's sheets. Neal hasn't done any business in a year and a half. He becomes irritated because he can't get new issues and calls in regularly at statement time. How does a broker fire this type of client? His stocks are quietly ordered out and he is placed on the third team.

ARE YOU ON YOUR BROKER'S FIRST, SECOND, OR THIRD TEAM?

It may come as a surprise, but the size or activity of an account does not always dictate whether you are on the first team. A broker feels more rewarded by instant response.

Someone who has said, "Look, my account is small, but when you get something, give me a call and I'll go along with you," will qualify for the first team. First-team members are experienced in Open-Air and feel free to bring Open-Air ideas to their brokers. Actually, everyone benefits because the broker might hear a great idea and share it with everyone. Without divulging names of clients, there can be a very profitable interchange of ideas. Active accounts and loyalists are first-team members. Million-dollar accounts that don't do business might be on the third team.

What are the advantages of being on the first team? In many instances, it pays to be notified quickly. A shocking world event can start a sharp correction, and the first five or six people called will benefit. They will be on the first team, not because of size, but probably because there is mutual trust, and the client won't need twenty minutes of explanation and interpretation. The broker knows he doesn't have to "sell him."

Conversely, the broker can get a wire from his firm recommending a stock, or see something on the tape, and the first five or six clients who get the news will profit the most.

In other words, first-team members have demonstrated their trust in their broker. Both parties are secure.

Second-team members might still be in the stage of needing their security blanket. The broker takes more time; he has to sell himself and his ideas. Second-team members may also be new accounts, so a breaking-in period is justified while they gain confidence. There can be an active $20,000 account on the first team and a new $2,000,000 account on the second team.

Some brokers segregate their teams by what is called their "book." Muni-bond buyers who want to be alerted on any new offerings can be on the first team along with active stock and option traders. Clients who want utility or bond offerings on a no-commission basis might also be on the first or second team. Brokers move their clients from "book" to "book" according to events. When time rewards instant decision, the broker won't call someone he thinks has lost confidence in him, nor will he call someone who hasn't gained confidence in him to begin with.

THE FIRST SIGNS OF BROKER-CLIENT DETERIORATION

Gary Good-Account had a $100,000 account and had done business with the same broker for six years. Every year he had made money and had also referred two other accounts to his broker. In February 1980, just before the March massacre, Gary was sitting on 500 shares of BanCal Tri-State, not an Open-Air stock, but one his broker had recommended as undervalued and also a buy-out candidate. The broker also put several other clients into the stock. The stock was 45, very active, and rumors were around that it was a take-over. Gary's cost four months earlier was 23. Gary was a member of the first team.

A brief statement by BanCal appeared on the tape: "We are in no discussions with anyone, nor are we interested in being acquired." As he did with other clients holding BanCal, the broker quickly called Gary, told him of the news, and said, "Let's get out." Gary, surprisingly, said, "Let me think about it." The stock started down and Gary finally sold it at 29 on its way to 21, losing 16 points. In addition, he sold other stocks as a result of the momentum that was then building during the March decline. Gary was always more *market-oriented* in his decisions than *individual-stock-oriented*. Nevertheless, the market plummeted. While Gary was late in his selling, he was glad to be out. Then tragedy struck! The broker could never get him back in.

Gary missed the entire 200-point upsurge from April to August. After many phone calls, the broker finally realized that Gary was paralyzed and getting more irritated at looking bad. He quit returning the broker's calls. Gary was placed in the second book—no sense calling anymore. Let him call the broker.

Like ballplayers, brokers get into slumps. Stocks they sell go up and the ones they buy go down. But like ballplayers, they can't stop coming to the plate. "A broker is only as good as his last suggestion" and "What have you done for me lately?" are vivid descriptions of the double-barreled pressure: the pressure of commissions plus the pressure to be right.

The worst thing that can happen to clients is if their broker loses *his* confidence. It might be one particular client who tips the scale, but to be of value to anyone, the broker must always feel like grabbing for the phone. I saw several brokers become comatose in the 200-point surge after Bunker Hunt day. They didn't believe it! As a result, they were not even passing on some very profitable recommendations from their firm. In this instance, no one prospered; the brokers made no commissions, and the clients did not improve their net worth.

Slumps take different forms. You can be right about the market and wrong about the groups you own. You can be out of a stock waiting for a correction, only to have it continue upward. You can buy defense stocks and the next day have the Russians request detente. You can buy a drug stock and next day have one of the company's drugs kill someone.

The deterioration accelerates, and the client starts to pick his or her own stock, only once in a while taking a courtesy recommendation from the broker. It has happened to every good broker, and generally the slump passes. If the relationship has been profitable before, it will resume. *Unless* . . . the client starts vocalizing that his or her picks are outperforming the broker's. The old "my stocks are doing better than yours," echoed by either client or broker, can start the deterioration fast. Too many I-told-you-sos can get the client fired. Brokers will sometimes forgo commissions in exchange for peace of mind.

MORE CANDIDATES FOR FIRING

Frankie Fairweather was a good account—until the March 1980 six-week drop ending on Bunker Hunt day. "I should have known better. My charts all said the market was going down, but I listened to you and now I've lost $17,000!" Mount St. Helens had erupted.

Frankie was also a new account, one who had jumped over from his previous broker after the October 1979 plunge. Quickly he generated several paper gains coming out of that distressed period, and he thought his broker was a hero. They were still holding onto the gains when the market topped out in February. "You didn't get me out, and from now on, I'm not listening to you. I'll make the decisions." Can *this* marriage be saved?

No! Get a divorce! A client who can't have confidence in his broker can't make it, and a broker doesn't need fairweather investors. The broker is now reduced to not calling his client because he knows he will be second-guessed. It is this type of situation that causes a broker to start rooting against his client. In the above example, for instance, Frankie had not *lost* $17,000; he had lost all the paper profits thus far accumulated. This is no longer the kind of client that a good broker might call on a weekend or a holiday with good or bad news.

William Well-Off had been with his broker for two years and had never taken a loss—eight trades, all at profits.

His portfolio had risen from $28,000 to $41,000. In addition, he had received another $2,500 in dividends. But now the market had been roaring ahead for three months, and William was doing all right, but he wasn't in oils, Computervision, or MA/COM. "I've seen better performance in a 5½% passbook savings account." "You've got me in bonds, not stocks! These damn things never move. The market's up ten and I'm up an eighth."

The broker had suggested sitting tight during the decline and even discouraged William from selling, but the irritation was building. The broker had experience in market rotation. He knew that not everything starts up at the same time and that the client would suffer once he started jumping from one stock to the next. What they sold would go up, and what they bought would go down. When the broker explained this to his client, they settled on a partial exchange from slow-moving stocks to "hot" stocks. The broker wasn't intimidated, nor did he *dictate* to his client. No one was fired.

Ricky Renege is a client who might be fired in a hurry. "Buy me 500 Ampex," says Ricky. Five days later the stock must be paid for, but Ampex is down a point and no check has arrived.

"We haven't received your check for Ampex."

"What Ampex? I only asked you what you thought of it. I didn't say buy!"

The broker knew he'd been had. This is a business where the individual broker must make good out of his own pocket on any such discrepancies. There are cases of brokers working off $20,000 and $30,000 losses as a result of being "bagged" by clients. In the above case, the firm busts the trade by selling the 500 Ampex with a one-point loss, and the broker gets a paycheck minus $500. But Ricky Renege is sued by the broker and the firm for the loss, plus damages. His name is also circulated among other brokerage firms, and Ricky takes his place on a "wanted poster" in the compliance department of all firms. Since the entire industry is built on a person's word (no contracts are signed between broker and client or between floor brokers on the New York Stock Exchange), a reneger's name gets top priority in all brokerage firms.

Lucy Late-Payment is a candidate for firing. New York Stock Exchange rules say that you must pay for your stock in five business days. The rule further states that in a one-year period a client may be granted an extension of two days on three separate occasions. After that, the client's account is frozen, meaning that a member firm must have her money on deposit before making a purchase, or must have stock delivered before making a sale. The New York Stock Exchange has a computer surveillance department, which monitors all firms on how they supervise this problem. Lucy just couldn't remember to pay for stock and, after the fourth late payment, her account was frozen.

Buy-on-the-High Harry is a candidate not necessarily to be fired, but one who should be placed in the third book and allowed to make his own decisions. He is referred to as one out of four—always reducing his broker down to where he gets his fourth choice and on the high.

"Buy Amerada Hess at 58."
"I'll watch it."
"Buy Exxon at 68."
"I'll watch it."
"There's bad news on your Itel."
"I'll think about it."
"Remember we talked about Goodyear, I have some news . . ."
"I'll wait for a pull-back."
"You know that Amerada Hess is moving."
"Where is it?"
"61."

"Who do you think shot J.R.?"
"Amerada Hess hit a big well in the North Sea."
"Where's the stock?"
"65."
"Buy me 300."

(One month later)

"Where's Amerada?"
"Backed off to 62."
"Why do I always buy the high?"

In summary, obvious troublemakers, renegers, or those who do no business are candidates to be fired. Many brokers will terminate a client who gives a lot of business but even more headaches. The office manager generally transfers those "difficult" accounts to rookies who need the business. Branch managers have been known to ask clients to take their business elsewhere.

Broker: If you want another good sign that this market decline is over, it's the fact that my first-team book is not keeping up with my inactive book.
Schwartz: No one likes you anymore?
Broker: Several former active accounts have said they are out of the market for a while—going to wait for a correction, so I change them over to inactive.
Schwartz: You mean they are fired?
Broker: Oh no, just inactive: third team. They're ones I just can't seem to convince about this market, so I'm not calling or sending anything. Inactive can also mean they've moved or died.
Schwartz: What's the definition of an active client?
Broker: Well, I had a surgeon call me once just before he went into surgery.

Schwartz: How would you like to be the poor bastard on the table after you've just told the doctor he had a margin call?

Broker: Especially if he got the margin call in a hospital supply stock. But you asked for a description of an active client.

Schwartz: Who makes the most money, the first team or the second?

Broker: First team. They get the Open-Air ideas first and the most service.

(The next week)

Broker: 100%, do you take any advisory services?

Schwartz: No. I have a theory about who I take advice from, and that's simply always to deal in person. Anyone can write after the fact.

Broker: It's like hitting on the driving range versus playing the big course.

Schwartz: Most never reveal what they are doing in their own account, and it's easy to engage in mail-order recommendations. Putting it in writing and saying "I told you so" doesn't make me any money. I don't find Open-Air in the mail!

Broker: Well, brokerage firms make recommendations.

Schwartz: Yeah, but it's you who has to live with your clients day after day, after passing on the recommendation. How would you like to have bought 1,000 shares of Day Mines at 33 on the advice of an advisory service and had to wait for the next weekly edition to find out why it went to 25 in one day?

Broker: Schwartz, you place a lot of credence in dealing with someone who also invests his own money in the market. There are a lot of capable brokers who might not have the financial capability to be in the market.

Schwartz: If they are so capable, they can afford it. It's a matter of belief. I want to deal with someone who has his own dough up. Anyway, with the possible exception of the *Professional Tape Reader*, I haven't found many advisory services with a prolonged good record.

Broker: In reality, advisory services are census takers; many of them give their readers what they want to hear. They don't lead, they follow. Look at the record—most of them have missed the important turns in the market.

Schwartz: There's even an advisory service called *Investors Intelligence*, which tracks all the advisory services and . . .

Broker: When most of them turn bearish, *Investors Intelligence* puts out a buy signal. Advisory services can be a lot like economists.

Schwartz: Paul A. Samuelson once compared economists to six Eskimos sleeping in a single bed. "If one rolls over, you can be sure the others will." Even Howard Ruff and Jim Dines made out by being doom-and-gloomers. Putting food in the basement, revolutions, stock market crashes and depressions—preaching all that stuff that never materialized. Nevertheless, it made them rich.

Broker: I've never made any money for anyone on the short side. In fact, one time I was right in predicting a market decline and got everyone out. The market dropped about 30 points, and then I couldn't get them back in. The damn thing went up 250 points and they missed the whole move.

Schwartz: Which of your clients are doing the best lately?
Broker: Well, I've got two little old ladies who are getting rich, and you're not doing so bad.
Schwartz: Two little old ladies?
Broker: Yes, I took down some Beldridge Oil and couldn't get anyone to buy it—even you didn't want it—so I put it in their accounts. Remember, it was $250, and eighteen months later Shell Oil paid $3,650 for Beldridge. Next, I took down 1,100 shares of Atwood Oceanic. Again nobody wanted it, so I put it in the same little old ladies' accounts. They got it last month at 28½, and now it's 39.
Schwartz: Same old story of what's tough to sell is probably the winner. Do you make it a practice of knowing what the other firms are recommending?
Broker: Definitely. It's called being aware of sponsorship. An Open-Air stock pick is generally early, but the sponsorship follows. The Toscos, Computervisions, Gulf of Canadas, and Wainocos all had the street behind them. You know, lots of young brokers get a good idea, come in all charged up, and get rejected on their first five calls. Then they stop on the stock. It might be they have another Tosco about to go from 5 to 30, but aren't telling the story right. An awareness of a lot of other opinions is necessary.
Schwartz: I like my broker to lead, not follow. It's been my experience that the best brokers are not easily swayed by the opinions of others.
Broker: You're right. But I'm talking about the initial stage of deciding whether to buy the stock or not. You need all the input you can get. After that, it's be aware, but be disciplined. A client who can lead the broker all over the lot saying

"Hell, let's get out, this thing isn't moving" finally gets the broker to relent. Then one day the client says, "I've got to get another broker; your timing is terrible."

Back to Open-Air. GM is a great buy here at 42. Detroit is a problem and whoever is the next president will have to deal with that. You know how Open-Air likes to spot problems?

Schwartz: I know, and I should probably take a tax loss on my Ford and Sears and buy General Motors. But I've got some time left before the end of the year.

(Three days later)

Schwartz: You got me off the john to tell me you think the market's going to hell?
Broker: We're down another 15—having an "oh-my-god, Carter-might-get-elected" market. Gold is down the limit, interest rates are higher. The Dow is heading back down to that 920 level again.
Schwartz: Buy into weakness and sell into strength! How's everything holding up?
Broker: Your oils are still strong. And the only ones that are down are Ford and Sears. Remember Genentech? It's down to 45 from 89!
Schwartz: I may be in trouble on Ford and Sears.
Broker: Well, Sears keeps reporting down retail sales, but Ford seemed to have good reception on the Escort.
Schwartz: I've visited four Ford dealers and three Sears stores on an Open-Air field trip, and it doesn't look good. Interest rates keep sneaking up, which could shut off new-car sales.
Broker: Plus the fact that a compact car with everything is over $8,000.

Broker: Squibb is 26 and Procter & Gamble is 68. But your Open-Air should carry you one step further. Get out of Procter & Gamble and into Johnson & Johnson.

Schwartz: Why?

Broker: When the TSS news broke, Johnson & Johnson turned strong because they are strong in sanitary napkins—Stayfree maxi-pads—rather than tampons.

Schwartz: Now who's using Open-Air? What price is Johnson & Johnson?

Broker: 79 3/8. One more Open-Air—you should take a look at Kimberly-Clark at 50; same deal with Kotex, but I hear they have a diaper that's giving Pampers of Procter & Gamble fits. It's called Huggies.

Schwartz: Okay, sell 300 each of Squibb and Procter & Gamble and split it between Gerber and Johnson & Johnson. Let me check on the Huggies thing on my next Open-Air field trip. Meanwhile, send me something on Kimberly-Clark.

Broker: That will give us 500 Gerber and 200 Johnson & Johnson. Well, Schwartz, the election's only a few days off. What's your Open-Air say?

Schwartz: If you interpret the mood of the people by what's been appearing on the best-seller list, and if you've noticed the craze for country-and-western music, then you've got to go with Reagan. Sounds crazy, but Open-Air doesn't always make sense in the beginning.

Broker: Hell, that Tony Lama boots has doubled for you. Reagan wears a cowboy hat, and everyone wants one.

Schwartz: Books like *Free to Choose, A Time for Truth, Restoring the American Dream, Crisis Investing,* and *How to Prepare for the Coming Bad Years* reflect the concern of a nation. The country at last is becoming financially and economically curious. That's enough for a change.

Broker: Well, even if Reagan wins, these interest rates are going to crunch one more time—perhaps a November massacre.

11

TIPS ON MANAGING YOUR PORTFOLIO

(DOES IT EVER PAY TO PANIC?)

At the end of 1975, Larry Long-Term bought 1,000 Memorex at 8 on his broker's recommendation. Five months later it was 30, and the broker called Larry to tell him he had sold his own stock and was also taking all of his clients out. Larry said he would watch it.

Almost seven months later, the broker called and reiterated the sale suggestion. The stock was still around 32, but Larry was not quite long-term. He said he would watch it. At 60 the broker no longer mentioned Memorex. Larry was a hero. What the hell was the broker doing, getting out at 30?

In 1978, at 45 and on the way down, Larry called the broker. "What do you think of Memorex now?"

"What can I say? I've been wrong on the damn thing—I thought it was overpriced at 30." At this point, both broker and client had forgotten that the broker picked the stock in the first place at 8.

"Put in a sell order at 50, good till canceled," advised Larry. "Done," said the broker.

A few months went by, and Larry called again. This time Memorex was 30. "Cancel the sell order at 50 and put it in at 40, good till canceled."

Throughout 1979, at 25 on Memorex, the customer's sell order was 35. At 20, the sell order was 25. At 15 Larry placed his last limit order, because an event was to occur that ended his agony: Bunker Hunt day on March 27, 1980. The first telephone line to light up that day was Larry Long-Term. "Sell it: we're crashing!" He got the low of the day just before the market firmed—10.

The whole adventure took three and a half years. He had a profit at one time of $52,000 after only putting up $8,000. He wound up with $9,800. Larry is now a broker, figuring he won't make those mistakes again. But a lot of costly mistakes are made on greed. If greed and fear played a tennis match, greed would win a tie breaker in the third set. Brokers have more disagreements with their clients in bull markets than in bear markets. Recommend a stock at 35 and have it go to 30, and clients are forgiving—almost fatalistic. They even console the broker. But recommend a stock at 35, get out of it at 45, and have it go to 60 . . . watch out—especially if you do that several times. All of a sudden you have cloned another Larry Long-Term. "By God, I've sold three straight stocks that all went up 20% after I sold them. From now on I'm going to hold long term." And then they get cut off at the knees. Buying a stock at 20 and selling it at 40 only to see it go to 50 is a profitable mistake. You never lose what you didn't have—and you didn't have the 10 points from 40 to 50. But, taking the same example, only riding the stock back down to 30 from 50 is something to lose—because you had those 20 points, they were yours.

Managing your own portfolio is nothing more than discipline. Discipline tends to neutralize the peaks and valleys of greed and fear. It's a case of designing a system that keeps you from being overly fearful or greedy at the wrong time. For instance, you would want your broker to adopt an attitude of eventually putting himself out of business where your portfolio is concerned. Get the portfolio into shape with the end result that you might make only six or seven trades a year. However, the size of the portfolio has an influence here. Someone thirty-five years old with $25,000 in the market trying for $100,000 will be more aggressive and have more trades than a retired person with $200,000 portfolio.

Why would a broker want to put himself out of business by getting your portfolio to the point of an occasional trim? Simple—for referrals, and professional self-satisfaction.

SOME OTHER POINTERS ON PORTFOLIO MANAGEMENT

Theoretically, the most activity in a portfolio should occur after a steep drop or a rapid rise in the total market. At bottoms, portfolios should decrease in their number of issues, because one needs always to ask oneself: of the 20 stocks I own, which would I buy here? Averaging down and buying more of certain stocks you own should take priority over turning to new issues. This discipline results in getting rid of bad stocks and adding to good ones at *bottoms* of markets. You then ride the next advance with little or no activity, but with a consolidated portfolio—more shares and fewer positions. At tops, you start to diversify the portfolio.

Since we never really know tops or bottoms when we're looking at them, the law of reason takes over. If a market has advanced 200 to 250 points, it might still have another 100 points to go, but it's far better to start moving $100,000 at this point from 7 or 8 issues to about 10 or 12 issues.

Most people do the reverse! After a big 200-point decline, in which their portfolio has lost 30%, they say, "Let's diversify so that never happens again." Then the market goes up 25%, and because they are spread all over the lot at the bottom, their portfolio increases only 15%. The overdiversified investor qualifies for that expression, "My stocks are holding well in an *up* market."

Basically, there should be only four reasons to change a portfolio:

1. To upgrade income
2. To consolidate at bottoms
3. To diversify at tops
4. To take action on an individual issue because:
   The stock has bad news.
   The stock has reached your price objective.

So one commandment for your own portfolio management is: *Have discipline during very emotional movements in the market.* In most cases, you should actually be going in the opposite direction of the emotion. For example:

The day after Reagan's election, we had an all-time record 84-million-share day, with the Dow once up 30 points. Selling into that strength was rewarding. In fact, the market fell back from there almost 30 points before starting another three-week rise of almost 70 points to 1,000 in the Dow. There was over a week to sell into that strength while it tried to penetrate 1,000. Subsequently, the market fell 100 points in ten trading days.

During the emotional down days of October 1978 and 1979, as well as Bunker Hunt day, it paid to be a buyer, not a seller. When Kennedy was shot, the market was so bad on the downside they suspended trading; it paid to be a buyer. The market opened up the following Monday and continued strong for several years.

Perhaps most difficult of all is to guard against the big loss. Remember, when you have a 50% decline, you need a 100% increase to make it up. What's that again? For example:

You buy a stock at 20 and it falls to 10—that's a 50% decrease. What do you then need in order to get even? That's right, it must double, or have a 100% increase. Experience teaches that stocks go from 20 to 10 much faster than they go from 10 to 20. "The Lord giveth and the Lord taketh away—but he taketh away faster than he giveth."

Should there be times when it is profitable to panic? Yes. Most of the time it involves individual stock situations like:

Itel	bankruptcy
Auto Train	bankruptcy
White Motor	bankruptcy

But there are times when Open-Air Analysis identifies a major event that has long-term implications for certain segments of our society.

For example:

When the Arabs first initiated the oil embargo in 1973, it was to have devastating ramifications for the RV (recreational vehicle) industry. The hot stocks at that time were Winnebago, Fleetwood, and Redman. Within the next two years they had fallen as follows:

	1972	1973	1974
Winnebago	48	27	2
Fleetwood	49	26	3
Redman	37	23	3

More recently, the Canadian government announced it was nationalizing 25% of the holdings of American oil companies. From the day of that announcement, this was the performance of oil companies with holdings in Canada:

	10/1/80	12/30/80
Dome Petro	67	59¾
Gulf Canada Ltd.	25⅝	19¾
Intercity Gas	19½	12¾

How much should you own of a particular stock? This can be answered only in down markets. If buying 1,000 shares of a $30 stock makes you uncomfortable when it drops to 25, then buy 500 or 200—whatever it takes to overcome panic when it's down. Here's what happens:

> One investor buys 1,000 shares at 30, becomes nervous at 25, and blows it out. Another investor who bought 500 at 30, but who is comfortable with it at 25, also thinks better at 25. He may have the agility to buy another 500 at 25 and reap the rewards a year later with the stock at 40. A nervous investor with an *uncomfortable position* might also make the mistake on the upside. The stock goes from 30 to 32, and he blows it out. Too many investors complain, "Why is it that when I own 100 shares, it goes up 20 points and when I own 1,000 it does nothing?" Take the "FF test" —when you fret over a fluctuation, you've got too much. Start with what's comfortable and work up with your position, not down.

MISSING A MARKET CAUSES YOU TO DO TWO THINGS WRONG

Remember, remember, remember: the best time to buy is generally when you're most frightened. Since most of us don't possess that discipline, we become "armchair millionaires."

The first thing to go wrong is that a stock market starts to move without us. We have our eye on a couple of stocks we want to buy "when the time is right."

The second thing to go wrong is that we drop down to our third or fourth choices when the market has moved and our first and second choices have also gone too far. Portfolio management can be reduced to these simplistic terms. Every three or four months, look at your holdings and say, "What is in my portfolio that is still my first choice?" Buy more of it, or replace a turkey with that one stock that truly is your first choice but has always looked too high.

DON'T PLACE TIME LIMITS ON YOUR INVESTMENTS

"I'll go with 25,000, but I need the money in two months."

A broker will respond to this by either putting you into utilities or going for broke trying to look good in a hurry—and he will probably succeed with your money . . . by going broke.

WHAT ABOUT KEEPING STOCKS IN STREET NAME?

Helen Hold-Your-Own walked into a brokerage office one day and said, "Sell my 1,000 Atlas." It was 17, and she had entered escrow on the purchase of a condominium thinking she had the use of $17,000. The broker sold the stock and five days later sent her a check for approximately $17,000. The plot thickened. She didn't really have 1,000 shares, only 200! It seemed that four years ago, Atlas had a 5-for-1 reverse split. Helen was to have exchanged her certificate for 1,000 shares and receive back from the transfer agent a certificate for 200 shares. Helen had moved around a lot, keeping her own stock in her possession. She never received the notice from Atlas about the reverse split. The transfer agent for Atlas Corporation detected the error when the brokerage firm delivered her 1,000 shares, to be redelivered to the buyer. Helen had to pay back about $13,500 and cancel her condo. This would never have happened if her stock was in street name. In street name, splits are handled automatically, and notices of tender offers are sent to clients with copies to their brokers.

Harry Hold-Your-Own walked into a brokerage office one day and said, "Sell my 25 U.S. Plywood 10¼ of 1990 converts. Last I saw, they were 120." Wrong! U.S. Plywood called those convertibles six months ago, and the best Harry could get was 105—the call price. He was out of the country and, because he held his own bonds, missed the notice from the company and could not sell the bond at the higher price or even convert to the underlying common stock. It cost him $3,750. This would not have happened had he had his bonds in street name.

Simply speaking, *street name* refers to the physical holding of your certificates by the brokerage firm. Securities Investor Protection Corporation (SIPC) insures all accounts up to $300,000, and most brokerage firms go one better and increase this figure to $500,000, with up to $100,000 of that amount applying to any cash balance in your account.

The single greatest advantage of street name accounting is that you receive the equivalent of a portfolio review every month. It's a way to measure the performance of your broker and your portfolio. Ask someone who holds his own stock how he has done in the market in the last several years: unless he is good at comparative mathematics, he won't know.

WHAT ABOUT MARGIN?

Margin is not for the fainthearted. However, we buy houses on margin (10 or 20%), cars on margin (monthly payments), why not stocks at 50% margin? On 50% margin, if a stock has a 50% move, then you double your money. As they say about Columbus—he didn't know where he was going when he started, he didn't know where he was when he got there, he didn't know where he had been when he returned; and he did it all on borrowed money.

Margin customers do not have the benefit of the Truth in Lending law; there is no three-day cooling-off period during which margin customers can back out of a margin transaction. And a margin call is like a recall notice from General Motors: it gets you back into the showroom. But the similarity ends there, because you must meet the call with cash or securities, or the brokerage firm can sell you out!

Why buy stocks on margin and pay outrageous interest rates? Can you invest on margin and still stay ahead of inflation—after taxes? Let's see what happens assuming borrowing costs of 22% and an inflation rate of 15%. If a hypothetical investor making between $35,200 and $45,000 (43% tax bracket) buys $20,000 worth of XYZ with a dividend return of 6%, the following occurs:

- He puts down $10,000 (assuming 50% margin requirements).
- He buys 500 shares of XYZ at 39¼; with commissions included it comes to $20,000.
- The borrowed $10,000 from the brokerage firm costs him 22%.
- His goal is to hold the stock for one year and one day to qualify for a long-term capital gain, and to beat inflation.

Interest charges will cost $2,200, but only $1,254 after taxes. Dividends will be $1,175, but only $669.75 after taxes. At this point, he is out $584.25 ($1,254 − $669.75) before taxes and inflation. So how high does the stock have to move before the whole thing is worthwhile?

- If inflation is 15%, he must make $1,500 on his $10,000 investment *plus* the $584.25 for a total of $2,084.25.
- After commissions on the liquidation and a 17.2% capital gains tax for his particular bracket, the gain would have to be $2,868.
- This represents a 14.34% gain on a $10,000 investment, or, simply, the stock would have to go from 39¼ to 45¾ in a year.
- If the inflation rate was only 10%, he would only need an increase of 11.3%.

The New York Stock Exchange composite index has risen at least 9% in seven of the last fourteen calendar years, and by 13% or more in five of them. Viewed in this light, the borrowing binge, even at 22%, doesn't seem quite so "incredible."

But what about the downside? What happens when you get the dreaded margin call? For illustration purposes, we will use higher-price stocks, because house calls (also known as maintenance calls) become more restrictive on lower-price stocks. The rule says that a brokerage firm can call you when your equity falls below 30% of your market value. For example:

You buy 500 shares of a $20 stock on margin. Your account looks like this after a deposit of $5,000, which represents 50% margin.

	MARKET VALUE	EQUITY	DEBIT (OWED TO FIRM)
500 shares of ABC @ 20	$10,000	$5,000	$5,000

ABC drops from 20 to 14. Now your account looks like this:

	MARKET VALUE	EQUITY	DEBIT (OWED TO FIRM)
500 shares of ABC @ 14	$ 7,000	$2,000	$5,000

What you owed the brokerage firm (debit balance) remained the same, and the market value dropped to $7,000 (500 @ 14); 30% of the market value is $2,100 and your equity is $2,000. So you get a margin call for ... $100.

In summary, consolidate your holdings after sizable market declines, and diversify your holdings after big gains. Always think first of buying more shares of what you already own rather than taking on an additional stock. Nowadays, it is more practical to keep your stocks with the broker in street name.

Broker: Okay, onward and upward.
Schwartz: How's your neck?
Broker: My neck?
Schwartz: From the whiplash of this market—Reagan's elected and we're up 15 on 84 million shares. The next day they raise the prime to 15½%, and they take the market down 17.
Broker: And now we've climbed all the way to 1,000 in the Dow. Shearson announced another split—3 for 2.
Schwartz: A split is one way Wall Street has of making division look like multiplication.
Broker: Don't knock it, you're getting rich. In fact, this market must be looking out into 1982, because they've got the prime rate back to 17½%; and T-bills are up to 15½%, and the market keeps going.
Schwartz: I hope like hell we aren't about to have another March 1980. Déjà vu.

Broker: As Nelson Bunker Hunt experienced—stock markets never take prisoners, and the margin clerk is a communist.

Schwartz: Speaking of prisoners, that MGM fire was horrible! All those people trapped! Who makes sprinkler heads?

Broker: ATO and Kidde. ATO is 16½, and Kidde is 41. Probably the main beneficiary of a new awareness about sprinkler heads and smoke detectors would be ATO. It's A-rated and sells for 6 times earnings.

Schwartz: Let me dwell on it. Next, who is the biggest factor in soccer? Everywhere I drive these days I see kids playing soccer—boys and girls.

Broker: Your Open-Air is most perceptive on this one. Soccer is sweeping the country, and it has something going for it that football and baseball don't.

Schwartz: It's got the girls.

Broker: Right. The biggest play on this would be AMF, selling at 20. Did you ever look into Stride Rite? You know Sperry Top Siders and the preppie look? The stock's up to 21 from 16 where we were looking at it.

Schwartz: Never got a chance, but I've been checking your Open-Air story on Kimberly-Clark, and you're right on both counts. Huggies and napkins. Ratings don't mean that much, but it is A+ rated, and hell, I can make money in a blue chip. What's the price?

Broker: 50½. But they could earn $8.50 in 1981.

Schwartz: Let's get 400.

Broker: Okay, but I also have to tell you some bad news. I'm getting all the Open-Air danger signals.

Schwartz: Such as . . . ?

Broker: Such as I'm a hit at cocktail parties. Inactive accounts are calling in and asking, "What's hot?" *Wall Street Week*'s ten-year anniversary show had almost ten guest analysts, and they were all bullish. And to make matters worse, the stock market made the cover of *Newsweek* magazine.

Schwartz: A Mickey Mantle baseball card sold for $3,100; the Dow is 1,000; and Thanksgiving 1980 is approaching. I've been worried about a November massacre, but it might happen in December. So we have a 50-point correction—big deal! Go ahead with the Kimberly-Clark.

Broker: Interest rates, interest rates. Fed funds have hit 19% and T-bills are 16%. It's hard to believe they were 5.85% at the end of June. And the prime was 10¾%.

Schwartz: Morgan Stanley has indicated it's time to lighten up on oil holdings, and Russia has made a big discovery in Siberia.

Broker: You won't believe how they pounded some of these oils on that news. Your Standard of Indiana fell from 99 to 80 in two weeks. Union Pacific fell almost 20 in a week. In fact, this oil picture is beginning to disturb me. They get hit because of Canadian nationalization; now they get hit again because of some discredited discovery in Siberia.

Schwartz: I guess I have to bite the bullet on my two losers, Sears and Ford. It's time to admit a mistake, take a tax loss, and raise some cash for a better use of the money. Sell the Sears and the Ford. They will probably be big stocks in '81; in fact, wait—what's GM?

Broker: 43½.

Schwartz: Dammit, my Open-Air still says, "Why aren't there any gas lines with the Iran and Iraq war and now total deregulation under Reagan?" If there's a glut building up, I want to be *in* autos, not out of them. I want to be in airlines and chemicals—the things that consume oil. Anyway, buy 500 GM with that money, and let's watch this oil thing. I take a tax loss on Ford but stay in autos. Now give me a summary after the losses in Sears and Ford.

Broker: Well, you bought 500 Ford at 27¾ and another 500 at 24, so you had a short-term loss of about $7,000. On Sears, you bought 500 at 18 and sold it at 16 for a $1,000 loss. The Squibb you sold at 26 is now 26 and the Procter & Gamble you sold at 68 is now 69. Each one of these was 10 points higher just a few months ago.

Schwartz: Don't start that; you know what it leads to, and we've been all through that. Take it from the top—what about the stuff we bought back in March and April?

Broker: Okay...

Bought 1,000 Juniper: 600 at 15½ and 400 at 16, now 23. Paper profit $7,300.

Bought 100 Standard of Indiana at 100; it's split 2 for 1, so you now have 200 at 84. Paper profit $6,300.

Bought 100 Standard of Ohio at 91; it's split 2 for 1, so you have 200 at 75. Paper profit $5,900.

Bought 500 Knogo at 27¼; it's now 20½, but it split 2 for 1, so you have paper profit of $6,750.

Bought 200 Magnuson Computer on the offering at 20. It's now 36. Paper profit $3,200.

Bought 200 Sensormatic at 26; it's now 31, and also split 2 for 1. Paper profit $7,200.

Bought 500 Tony Lama at 7; it's now 15. Paper profit $4,000.

Bought 500 Eastman Kodak at 50; it's now 66. Paper profit $8,000.

Bought 1,500 MCI Communications: 1,000 at 5½, and 500 at 10⅛; it's now 13. Paper profit $8,900.

Bought 500 Shearson at 27. After 4-3 and 3-2 splits, you have 1,000 shares at 36. Paper profit $22,500.

Bought 1,000 Minnetonka: 200 at 8 and 800 at 12, before split. It split 2 for 1, and it's now 48. Paper profit $85,800. Schwartz, you're a hero! I'll say it before you do. I didn't like that stock at first.

Bought 500 MA/COM at 30. After a 2-for-1 split, you have 1,000 at 30. Paper profit $15,000.

Bought 500 Applicon: 200 at 22 and 300 at 32; it's now 45. Paper profit $8,000.

Bought 500 Gerber at 24; it's now 26. Paper profit $1,000. You're going to wish you owned more of this someday.

Bought 200 Johnson & Johnson at 80; it's now 95. Paper profit $3,000.

Bought 100 Waste Management at 62, and it's now 90. Paper profit $2,800.

Bought 1,000 Zenith at 14½, now 20. Paper profit $5,500.

Bought 500 Cooper Tire and Rubber at 11, now 28. Paper profit $8,500.

Just bought 400 Kimberly-Clark at 50½ and it's 51, and 500 GM at 43½. Incidentally, I believe so strongly in the theory that what's hardest for me to sell my clients is the best buy that I

	generally buy those hard-sells in my own account. I've just bought 100 GM myself. I've tried my fifteen best accounts, ones that almost always go along with me, and only one bought the idea.
Schwartz:	I may have to buy you a Christmas present.
Broker:	Keep it under $25, but you can give me an order anytime. Want to feel bad?
Schwartz:	No. What did I sell that went up 100%? Or what did I not buy that doubled?
Broker:	Your Open-Air Sun Belt package. Have you followed it? Mesa Petroleum, Tom Brown, Louisiana Land, Big Three and ...
Schwartz:	I hope you always keep reminding me of the ones I missed. Shows we're still in the groove. They never boo a bum.
Broker:	We've done business for a long time, but to keep things in perspective, remember the first order you gave me on Brunswick? Buy 100 shares at 12¾. You've come a long way, baby, because you just ran about $10,200 in Minnetonka to $96,000, and you're not even long-term yet. Why don't you write a book on Open-Air?
Schwartz:	I might.

(Several weeks later)

Broker:	Well, Schwartz, it was a December massacre—100 points in ten days. 90-day T-bills got to 17%; the prime is at 20%, and the London market has fallen from 508 to 457. Your 50-point correction was a bad one.
Schwartz:	Some of my big profits have become little profits. What's Open-Air say?
Broker:	Several things. The strength in GM through all this is interesting. Also, we have literally crashed

in commodities. For several weeks they have been collapsing.

Schwartz: Disinflation, disinflation. Volcker's high interest rates, the talk about Reagan's budget cuts, all the rebates on cars, and I've noticed some pretty good discounts on the sale of houses.

Broker: When you disinflate, you get out of oil, gold, and real estate and buy stocks, bonds, and cash.

Schwartz: Right. Back to the weakness in commodities. What did food stocks do in all this?

Broker: Held like a rock. Nabisco, Borden, Consolidated Foods, Kellogg, General Foods, Hershey Foods, even McDonald's, Denny's, and Safeway were strong. Your Gerber was even up slightly.

Schwartz: Well, we said there would be one more credit crunch—it will probably last through the first part of 1981.

Broker: Hey, Schwartz, you want a real Open-Air, I mean a *real* one?

Schwartz: Whisper, so no one will hear.

Broker: Actually, *Business Week* got my attention onto this back in the October 20 issue. With Reagan in and Carter out, you buy Hart Schaffner & Marx and sell Tony Lama boots!

Schwartz: It's such a natural! Just do it! I don't even want to hear the analysis. Don't screw me up with the facts. Wow! What a cocktail-party story.

Broker: Okay, I'll do it. The Tony Lama is still around 16, so you make $3,500, and Hart Schaffner is 12⅝. We can get around 600 shares. There's probably a little more left in Tony, but if you don't leave some for the other guy, he won't buy it from you.

Schwartz: Actually, the more I think about it, demography really justifies this move. The biggest segment of the population is twenty-five to forty-four years old, and they are the suit buyers.

Broker: The stock will earn $2.60 in 1980 and maybe $2.90 in 1981. Which will make its sixth straight year of earnings increases, so it's less than 5 times earnings and going into the lower-priced mass-market area, also women's wear.

Schwartz: Open-Air, where would we be without you?!

◀❰ 12 ❱▶

JOE GRANVILLE
AND THE INSTITUTIONS

(CAN OPEN-AIR BEAT THOSE GUYS?)

In late November 1980 the Dow Jones broke through 1,000. This was about the twelfth time it had done this since it first hit 1,000 in 1966. This time when the Dow reached the 1,000 level an ominous sign reappeared. The strength in the market was almost all in oil stocks. Just as quickly, the market dropped 100 points in ten business days, while Henry Kaufman's predictions of higher interest rates came true. The prime reached a record 21½%; Fed funds were 19%; and T-bills hit 18%. The Dow held around the 915 to 920 level and started back up—this time *without* the oils.

On Tuesday, January 6, 1981, the stock market had an inter-day high of 1,013 and a close of 1,004.69. That evening Joe Granville took off from his Florida headquarters and dropped a bomb on the New York Stock Exchange. Overnight he sent out telegrams to some of his subscribers saying to sell everything and also to go short the market.

On Wednesday, the Dow Jones at one time was down 31 points, and it ended the day being off 23.80. Total volume was a record 92,890,000, which broke the previous record of 84,297,350 on November 5, 1980, the day after Reagan was elected.

According to *Wall Street Journal* staff reporter Charles J. Elia, the overnight telegrams went to approximately 3,000 subscribers and were relayed to clients by 30 callers. An astounding impact! Never did so few do so much to so many. The tragedy of the situation was that approximately 10,000 of Granville's *other* subscribers were getting a wildly bullish letter saying, "Do some aggressive new buying." This letter was dated January 3, 1981. Why the abrupt switch? What sort of shape can a stock market be in to be that vulnerable? Why two-tier subscribers? Granville's reply: "We say right out in a legend printed on our letters that all opinions are subject to change without notice. We have to be true to our theory."

Dan Rather of CBS replied: "Looking at the effects of one man's opinion, Joe Granville, on the stock market—this isn't a bull market or a bear market, it's a sheep market." As for the two-tier subscribers, according to Alan Abelson of *Barron's*, the elite 5,000 who pay $500 a year for their subscriptions were being told to sell, while the other 10,000 who only pay $250 were being told, in an earlier standard letter, to buy.

In a January 1981 edition of *Forbes* magazine, an article by Newcomb Stillwell listed some of the horror stories of that day:

> Trading in Petro Lewis—with exchange approval—opened an hour late at 22½, down 10⅜. It closed that day at 24½ and opened the next day at 29¾.
> Prime Computer, also on a delayed opening, opened at 32½, down 6⅛ from the previous day. It closed at 36.
> Other stocks are shown on the next page with their opening prices (what most Granville subscribers were getting) and their subsequent closes:

	OPEN	CLOSE
GM	46¼	46⅝
Standard of Indiana	74½	76⅞
Standard of Ohio	62¼	68⅛

Said one New York Stock Exchange floor specialist, "Three or four times a year we have to put our wallets and houses and cars and the kids' education on the line. Wednesday was one of those days."

Who is Joe Granville? Maybe it is more appropriate to ask who *was* Joe Granville. First, he is a fellow with a mighty ego and an above-average record at calling *intermediate* market swings. He gained notoriety for being below average on stock selection. He is a member of the investment advisory mail-order crowd. If you subscribed, then you were a "Granville Groupie." After Granville's sell signal on January 7, 1981, the market retreated once again to about the 920 to 930 level. During this time, Granville received an assist from Henry Kaufman of Salomon Brothers, who again predicted higher interest rates to come in 1981. But the best both of them could do together was get the market down to a level about 20 points above the previous low. Granville's subsequent predictions that the market would fall below 900 did not materialize. As one Wall Street-wise professional opined, "Just when you think you've got the key to the market, someone changes the lock."

For the following month after his sell signal, Granville appeared on many programs, including *The Phil Donahue Show*. This show has a wide following and was, therefore, being seen someplace in the United States every day for the next eight weeks. It gave Joe a chance to make his point. Interestingly enough, as his exposure on this program began to fade into the smaller cities, the stock market started firming. An Open-Air awareness of how *The Phil Donahue Show* worked might have caused someone to initiate stock buying programs after the third week.

One of Granville's best-remembered recommendations was in his continuous bullish stance on the market from April 1973 to the end of 1974. While Joe kept saying "Buy," the market plunged almost 400 points.

Later, in February 1981, Granville made some other predictions:

1. Tomorrow the market will sell off 16 points (it rose 8).
2. By next year, I will win a Nobel Prize for cracking the mystery of the market.
3. On April 10 a major earthquake will happen in Los Angeles.

Perhaps an insight into the entire fiasco is best represented by the following exchange with Joe Granville during one of his interviews:

"Do you own stocks?" he was asked.

"No, I make $6 million a year from my advisory service."

Can an individual beat the Joe Granvilles and the institutions? In a gallop—in a warm-up—in straight sets, a shut-out!

Institutions have to play index funds; they can't really employ Open-Air, because much is done by committee. Furthermore, they are restricted to large-capitalization issues, so it is difficult to buy emerging growth companies over the counter with a small number of shares outstanding. Speaking of large institutional money managers, have you heard your kids say, "But Sandra (or Kenny) has one"? Would you believe that big institutions have "kids' day" four times a year? It's called portfolio window dressing and goes something like this:

> Peter Peer Group, the widely respected Boston money manager, doesn't want the rest of the street to see in the March 1980 quarterly report that he

still has a heavy position in utilities. Utilities have become sky divers in that high-interest period, and the only ones left holding them are little old ladies—not institutions, and especially not Peter Peer Group. So, on March 27, 28, and 29, it's a "gozinta." He gets out of utilities and gozinta oils.

Now, how in the world can a small investor be at the mercy of all of this? The men and women who run the huge portfolios (with other people's money) become tanks running all over the individual while he is looking for the land mines that populate the investing world. Just how are those Sherman tanks of institutions doing compared with us foot soldiers? Lousy! For example:

Mutual funds headed into 1981 loaded up on integrated domestic and international oils. Individual issues dominating the funds' buy lists were Royal Dutch, Texaco, Getty, Cities Service, and Union Oil. One of the weakest groups in the first four months of 1981 was oils!

Another example: when the market bottomed out in the fall of 1974, private pension funds were allocating a mere 20% of cash flow into equities. Again in the first quarter of 1978, the pension funds were putting almost no money into equities.

Anthony Hitschler, President of Provident Capital Management, an investment arm of Provident National Bank in Philadephia, says institutions "are too attracted to the industries and stocks with the best stories." Soon the entire institutional community is playing the same game. The mutual funds, insurance companies, and individual investment advisors end up paying too much for "story" stocks.

Institutions, like aircraft carriers, are slow to turn. They have committees, and committees don't practice Open-Air Analysis. It's the individual experienced in Open-Air who spots things right under his nose.

Is it an individual or a committee that might have noticed the popularity of the disposable razor by Gillette in late 1980?

Did individual ophthalmologists or a committee pick up on contact lenses and, hence, buy Bausch and Lomb or Continuous Curve?

Wouldn't individual architects and engineers discover Computervision before an institution would?

Every gas station owner, mechanic, and car dealer should have owned Safety-Kleen. They were the first ones exposed to the device, and the stock went from 8¼ on April 3, 1979, to 32 on April 17, 1981. It quadrupled in two years!

Stockbrokers *and* clients should have picked up on stockbrokerage stocks back in 1980. Volume was starting to build. An institutional committee might have made the buy recommendation *after* the stocks doubled.

Did individual doctors see right under their noses enough to buy SmithKline or Humana or National Medical? They would have seen it before anyone, especially an institution.

A new company called ISC Systems came public in late 1980 at 19½. It developed computer intelligence systems for the savings and loan, banking, and thrift industries. Its first few customers were West Coast savings and loans. There was a terminal for every teller, much like a Quotron for every stockbroker, but there are tens of thousands more S&L and banking tellers than stockbrokers. Would an institution see this potential at first? No, but everyone connected at those first savings and loan and banking institutions sure did. If any of these were Open-Air practitioners, they got rich watching the stock go to 70 in seven months!

Who is the first to notice a baby boom? A pediatrician, a mother, or an institution in Wall Street?

Let's look one more time at the institutional performance for the five-year period ending 1979. It should be noted that institutions, including mutual funds, fared very well for the single year 1980, but it's the five-year comparison that is meaningful.

COMPOUNDED ANNUAL RATES OF RETURN
(CAPITAL GAINS PLUS DIVIDENDS)*

Standard & Poor's 500	+14.7%
Dow Jones Averages	+12.0%
Salomon Brothers High-Grade Bond Index	+ 5.8%
Pooled equity funds of bank & insurance companies	+12.7%

To reiterate: pooled equity funds of bank and insurance companies plus pension funds did not beat the Standard & Poor's averages!

For the five-year period ending 1980, the figures* look like this:

Standard & Poor's	+13.9%
Dow Jones	+ 8.2%
Salomon Brothers High-Grade Bond Index	+ 2.4%
Pooled equity	+12.9%

And for the first quarter of 1981*:

Standard & Poor's	+ 1.3%
Dow Jones	+ 5.6%
Salomon Brothers High-Grade Bond Index	− 1.1%
Pooled equity	+ 2.0%

In the above cases, pooled equity funds beat the Dow for five years ending 1980, but did not better the more widely represented Standard & Poor's. In the first quarter, they

---

* Source: Bernstein-Macaulay, Inc.

finally defeated the Standard & Poor's, but not the Dow. The big guys are easy!

Broker: No wonder people take refuge in real estate. We hit 1,000 then drop 100 points in ten days, go back up to 1,000, and Joe Granville does his act. Now we're floundering around at 940, and the phones have stopped ringing again.

Schwartz: People are funny. They will buy a condo or house and have it increase 50% in two or three years and be ecstatic. They buy a stock, and if it hasn't done anything in two months, or if they've been subjected to what we just went through, they...

Broker: Throw in the towel and say, "The market's not for me."

Schwartz: If people woke up every morning to "The real estate 9:00 A.M. shopping center index is down 10; the apartment house index is down 7; and condos are unchanged," they would have the same emotions to deal with that we have.

Broker: How about buying condo futures or a closed-end fund of raw land? But Schwartz, I've got to tell you about an Open-Air test I gave to several other brokers and sophisticated people in December.

Schwartz: I'm taking notes.

Broker: I asked each individual to tell me (a) you're full of BS; (b) you're half right; or (c) you're right, to the following statement: the oils and high-technology stocks have topped out.

Schwartz: And...?

Broker: Everyone chose (a)—I was full of BS!

Schwartz: Well, we've been agonizing over this too long, and I've watched my oil profits turn to what they

	called you. My Open-Air says sell. There are no gas lines; the oils did not participate at all in that last run to 1,000 before Granville day, and...
Broker:	If you notice in the back of *Barron's*, crude inventories and gasoline inventories keep climbing. Then...
Schwartz:	All the talk of deregulation should cause better action unless...
Broker:	It's already discounted. Buy on anticipation and sell on reality. Foreplay makes all the money in the stock market. Remember Brunswick? Your Open-Air said sell when you could find an alley. Now you can find plenty of gas when there is supposed to be a shortage.
Schwartz:	Yeah, but what do we go into?
Broker:	Foods, drugs, airlines, autos. During this weakness in oils, it was obvious, just obvious!
Schwartz:	What was obvious?
Broker:	The oils were weak and the things that consume oil were strong.
Schwartz:	My Open-Air says start buying foods, with commodity prices going into the cliff.
Broker:	Let your broker make you do it. Get out of oils and into the following: Nabisco, Borden, Goodyear, and some chemicals.
Schwartz:	Why Goodyear?
Broker:	Same reason as GM. They're coming out of this more in control of their industry. Firestone is hurt and Goodrich has cut back.
Schwartz:	Okay, I'm still short-term on most of this, but let's get out of Juniper, Standard of Indiana, and Standard of Ohio, and buy Nabisco, Borden, General Mills and Goodyear. Let me know.
Broker:	We sold 1,000 Juniper at 19, 200 Standard of Indiana at 72, and 200 Standard of Ohio at 62.

Profits on Juniper were $4,700. Profits on Indiana were $5,000. Profits on Ohio were $4,000. We bought 500 Nabisco at 27, 400 General Mills at 30, 1,000 Borden at 26, and 500 Goodyear at 17. I know, we let about $10,000 in profit evaporate on us.

Schwartz: Well, Open-Air says Nabisco's got something in this new Wheatsworth cracker. I checked back to a *Business Week* article on Nabisco—in fact, it was the same issue as the one they did on Hart Schaffner & Marx. A lot of people still eat Oreos and Ritz crackers.

Broker: Does your Open-Air acknowledge they will be paying lower wheat prices?

Schwartz: You never know about commodity prices or the weather. Open-Air just says food stocks could go from 6 times earnings to 10 times earnings. Take General Mills. I'll bet no one realizes they own the Red Lobster, York Steakhouse, or Good Earth restaurant chains. Maybe their biggest winner is Wallpaper to Go—an interesting concept in merchandising wallpaper. I want to own this stock at 30.

Broker: Actually, I think the food group might be one of the few better-performing groups this year.

Schwartz: You sound like Granville.

Broker: If I ever agree with him, I'll turn in my stock guide. However, 1981 could be another 1977—an overall lousy market but with some very strong areas.

Schwartz: Okay, what's the punch line?

Broker: Let's play "What if?" What if Reagan gets his budget cuts and his tax cuts, but Volcker keeps interest rates high?

Schwartz: Then we get another recession; the market will

	probably have a good correction; and we will pick up some more cheap stock just like we did last spring. But why would interest rates stay up if Reagan's plan brings down inflation?
Broker:	That's the point. Volcker got egg on his face this last June when he let rates come down at the same pace with inflation.
Schwartz:	And we reheated inflation all over again.
Broker:	Right. I'm betting if they come down at all it will be agonizingly slow.
Schwartz:	That just might wipe out a few savings and loans and possibly other marginal companies like Pan American.
Broker:	And the cycle will happen again: advisory services will turn bearish; brokerage firms will turn bearish; clients will stop calling in; and the best indicator of a bottom will be my gross. It will tank. Gone will be the days of Grover!
Schwartz:	Grover?
Broker:	Grover Cleveland is on the thousand-dollar bill.
Schwartz:	Poor baby. When you start bringing your lunch, I'll start buying.
Broker:	There's my other phone. It might be Mr. *Really Big*.
Schwartz:	I thought I was Mr. Really Big.

13

OPEN-AIR ANALYSIS LOOKS AT PROFITS IN THE EIGHTIES

(WHAT MIGHT BE OBVIOUS IN 1982 AND 1983)

The most reliable way to get rich in the stock market is to own shares of companies with rising earnings and rising price earnings multiples.

The perfect environment for investing:

April 1978:	Inflation is accelerating.
June 1978:	Interest rates start rising.
July 1978:	Gold climbs above $200.
August 1978:	Dollar starts sliding.
October 1978:	The October '78 massacre; Dow drops 170.
November 1978:	OPEC raises oil prices.
April 1979:	Industrial output drops.
August 1979:	Prime rate hits 13%.
September 1979:	Another major Fed policy change.
October 1979:	OPEC raises oil prices.
October 1979:	Another October massacre; Dow drops 160.
November 1979:	Iran seizes hostages.
December 1979:	Russia invades Afghanistan.
January 1980:	Money supply keeps rising.
February 1980:	Uncertainty over election.
February 1980:	Gold hits $875.

March 1980:	Bunker Hunt crash; Dow drops 180.
April 1980:	Prime hits 20%.
May 1980:	Housing starts to collapse.
June 1980:	Car sales collapse.
June 1980:	Money supply and interest rates come down.
July 1980:	Money supply starts back up $9.7 billion.
September 1980:	Iraq/Iran war.
October 1980:	Carter/Reagan debate.
November 1980:	Reagan wins election.
December 1980:	Oils top out.
December 1980:	Dow drops 100 in 10 days.
January 1981:	Granville says sell.
January 1981:	Prime hits all-time high: 21½%.
February 1981:	Reagan starts fight against inflation.
March 1981:	Reagan survives assassination attempt.
April 1981:	Polish crisis.

It will be just as bad in the eighties. It *always* is. Waiting for the proper time to invest means never investing or, worse, when it appears to be the best time to invest, the Dow has already advanced 200 points. And as we have learned in the previous chapters, people got rich on the obvious during very uncertain times. Open-Air is not just a recent phenomenon.

Which historians can forget the fortunes made in Mead Johnson stock in the late fifties and early sixties when they bought out Metrecal? Or the people who retired on Syntex when it introduced the birth control pill? Levitz Furniture caught the eye of Open-Air analyzers in the early seventies when it demonstrated a new method of merchandising furniture. Even a can of oil called WD-40 made people rich! These obvious opportunities occurred during very uncertain times also—recessions, U-2 incidents, Kennedy-Nixon elections, or the war in Viet Nam.

What looks obvious in the eighties? Anyone connected with publishing knows that books are often completed a full six to nine months before publication, so forecasting here might be more than risky—it might be stupid. As the saying goes, if you are going to forecast, then forecast often. Economists and stock market gurus can get away with that because we don't remember their last predictions. But in a *book*! Anyway, here goes.

The market is *not* a mirror of today's news. If it were, all you would need is a newspaper to make money. No one ever said making money was easy, but if we remember the three ingredients of Open-Air Analysis, namely:

1. Identify a problem
2. Detect a trend
3. Spot breakthroughs

then we can departmentalize our crystal ball. Let's start with number 2 first, detecting trends.

Perhaps the most controversial prediction made in this book is that—*the energy crisis will be over by 1985*. To quote from an article by S. Fred Singer in *The Wall Street Journal* on February 4, 1981:

> By the end of this decade, and certainly in the 1990s, the free world may require less than half of the oil it uses today: some 20 million barrels per day instead of 50 million barrels per day.
>
> Several factors will bring about these changes.
>
> 1. New coal technologies
> 2. Advances in refinery technology (producing more

light products: gasoline and motor fuels, and less heavy fuel oil from a barrel of oil)

3. The law of economics: higher oil prices encourage conservation

4. More efficient cars entering the market

We advance the estimate of self-sufficiency to 1985. Natural gas, as a result of deregulation, is being found in abundant quantities to serve as an oil substitute. Further, propane is becoming a very popular gasoline substitute. Cars are starting to run on propane. A February 1981 article in *Barron's* stated, "The rate at which fleets of conventional gas-fueled cars and trucks are being converted to run on propane makes a lightning romance seem downright possible."

So, together with the possibility of solving our energy problems by 1985, what does this contribute to further trends? It means having less inflation, lower interest rates, and higher productivity. The election of President Reagan, the mood of the country and of Congress, a new stirring in America toward capitalism and toward learning economics brings the observation that the eighties could be the space-age sixties. Religion, family, and marriage are *in*. So are the words *supply-side economics* and *disinflation*.

So if Open-Air detects a trend of disinflation, how do we convert that to profits in the stock market? Remember, we will be making a sea change, a slow turnabout in lifestyles from fighting inflation and a cheaper dollar to taking advantage of the fact that the dollar will buy *more*. It is particularly difficult for investors to make these transitions. They require monumental efforts. For example, a major transition occurred at the end of the sixties. *Because* of inflation, money started flowing out of stocks into real estate. Some people never made that transition. Could the same thing be happening for the eighties, only in reverse?

What suffers when disinflation occurs? The usual hedges

against inflation, such as gold, silver, oil, and real estate. What profits? Stocks, bonds, and cash! At the time of this writing, in early 1981, that very scenario is unfolding.

Of course, the script can change fast. A sudden seizure of the Strait of Hormuz by a foreign power can send oils and gold shooting up while the rest of the market collapses.

Under disinflation, there are generally lower commodity prices, which Open-Air concludes is bullish for food companies. When food companies are able to buy their raw material more cheaply, their profit margins rise, and the price of their stock is likely to follow. Some of these companies are Gerber, Nabisco, Borden, Consolidated Foods, Hershey, General Mills, and Quaker Oats. Under disinflation, there is a stronger dollar, and with a stronger dollar comes a willingness to plan ahead. Consumers will come into their own in the eighties, as will American cars and homebuilding.

A house in the eighties might be regarded as it was in the sixties—a consumer item. Homebuilding companies like Lennar, U.S. Home, Kaufman & Broad, U.S. Plywood, and Georgia Pacific will participate. We will probably witness a comeback in mobile homes and savings and loans. We can't stop "pent-up demand." Remember what happened in real estate between 1975 and 1980?

And the decade of the eighties will see the comeback of the American car! The number of cars on the road over four years old is at a record high. If you believe the price of gasoline will top out at $1.50 to $1.60 per gallon, then the eighties may be the year of General Motors and Ford, in that order. Open-Air says if it's big in autos, it's got to be big in tires also. Goodyear gets the clear nod. If ever two companies were emerging from the ashes clearly in charge of their industries, it's General Motors and Goodyear.

Demography will be important to investors in the eighties. The largest group of our society will be between twenty-five and forty-four. In this age span, for the most part, ultimate lifestyle decisions are made. This group appears to be adopting more traditional values. Consumer appliances, furniture, homes, baby food, and clothes will be the beneficiaries. Almost half of all births in the eighties will be first births, and substantially more money is spent on the first child. This will benefit a company like Gerber. Other consumer companies like Sunbeam, GE, Levitz, and Magic Chef will be typical of those participating in the rebirth of the consumer. Perhaps most explosive of all will be consumer high technology. By 1983 the average family might have two cars, three televisions, one food processor, and a *home computer*.

Home banking, home stock market analysis, home reading of the newspaper, and home shopping will all be done through the computer. The TV is the center and the computer will be attached to it. RCA has already spent more money on video discs than it took to bring color TV to the market twenty-five years ago. It is estimated there will be 5 million videodisc players sold by 1990. A lineup of companies that will participate in the area of home technology includes

Apple Computer	MGM
CBS	Oak Industries
Commodore International	RCA
General Electric	Tandy
MCA	Zenith

Finally demography will focus on three trends already in their infant stages: the popularity of high-class health food restaurants, the rise of legal clinics, and the importance of day-care centers. Day-care centers in the eighties will be as necessary as nursing homes were in the seventies.

There is an old Wall Street adage that says there are more antitrust breakups under Republicans than there are under Democrats. IBM, American Telephone, and General Motors are prime candidates. And all these qualify for that old geometry expression, "The sum of the parts is *greater* than the whole." Open-Air analysis says that instead of buying a stock and hoping a large company takes it over, buy GM, American Telephone, and IBM and hope they're broken up into smaller pieces. All three stocks should go up on any breakup news.

In fact, it's interesting to step back in the open air and take a look at these three companies. Only GM has no *new* competition chipping away at it. The Japanese threat might actually diminish by the 1983 model year because, reportedly, GM expects its mid-size cars (Pontiacs, Buicks, and Oldsmobiles) to be getting 28 miles per gallon in the city, which is what subcompact cars, including Japanese, get in 1981. Further, there are the voluntary export cutbacks by the Japanese.

American Telephone has all kinds of competition chipping away and taking parts of its domain. Companies include

Continental Telephone	Telecom Equipment
Graphic Scanning	Telecommunications
MicomSystems	TIE Communications
MCI Corporation	TII Industries
Radiofone	Universal Communi-
Rolm	cation System
Southern Pacific	Western Union

The name of the industry has even changed. It's not the telephone industry anymore, it's the telecommunications industry. The range of services to phone users is about to explode. There are "phone stores" now, just as there are "computer stores." The interconnect industry—the core formulation of the office of the future—connecting telephones to computers to TVs, and computer to computer is part of this burgeoning new industry.

Perhaps the fastest-growing segment of the telecommunications industry will be a new subgroup referred to as "information vending." Walk up to a bank or savings and loan teller and get information on your account out of an ISC terminal. Walk into your broker's or insurance agent's and get information out of a Quotron system. Larger companies like Dun and Bradstreet, The New York Times, and American Express are involved in information vending. A manufacturer of the actual hardware might be a company like Zentec.

The number of companies fighting IBM is too long for publication, but, increasingly, separate industries like word processing, featuring Wang Laboratories, NBI, and CPT are beating IBM to the punch. Another new industry formed in the late seventies is the CAD/CAM industry, which means computer aid design and manufacturing. Companies like Computervision, Gerber Scientific, Applicon, Auto-trol, and Intergraph created that industry without interference from IBM. New specialty companies in computers like Network Systems, ISC, and SEI are also creating a new niche in the computer industry.

As for trends, it is particularly noteworthy to observe what's going on in England. At the time of this writing, all world economies are sluggish, but since the election of Margaret Thatcher, England has dropped her inflation rate from 28% to 12%. In fact, it dropped nine months in a row. England before Thatcher was much in the same position as the United States before Reagan. Countries take their turn with their own final spasms of troubled decades. England has turned the corner. During this period of disinflation, her stock market soared. The United States disinflation process probably began in the spring of 1981.

So Open-Air concludes the "detecting trends" segment by predicting declining oil prices, declining inflation rates and declining interest rates through the eighties. That means a transition from oil, collectibles, gold, silver, diamonds, and real estate into stocks, bonds, and cash. In this environment, the Dow Jones could reach 12 to 15 times earnings, or near 1,600 by 1985. As we have just learned, Open-Air makes money by detecting trends, spotting breakthroughs, and detecting problems—not predicting markets. But since everyone on *Wall Street Week* talks about "the market," we will play that game, too. For what it's worth!

Now, what about breakthroughs? For an Open-Air breakthrough, none is more far-reaching than gene splicing. It all started at General Electric. A GE scientist created a "bug" that could digest different parts of crude oil. The end result was an oil-eating device capable of cleaning up oil spills. GE applied for a patent in 1972, and the Supreme Court ruled in 1980 that companies could patent production of new bacteria and microbes developed through gene splicing.

What is gene splicing, or genetic engineering? It is that purposeful manipulation of genetic information within cells to mass-produce specific microorganisms. We have been using this principle to ferment wine, leaven bread, and ripen cheese. The central purpose of genetic engineering is to harness the ability of cells to produce chemicals. In other words, genetic engineers control, by alteration, the information coded in the genes in order to cause the cells to make products useful to humans.

Useful products? Human insulin and interferon for openers. Interferon is a new hope for fighting cancer. Genentech claims it has accomplished a breakthrough by producing interferon, a protein, from yeast. Yeast doesn't give off toxicity, which makes it easier for mass production. Other possibilities include:

1. Producing hormones to speed growth of cattle, hogs, and other animals
2. Producing vaccines against hepatitis and malaria
3. Producing high-fructose corn syrup
4. Converting corn-derived glucose to alcohol

5. Developing a substance to "push out" unrecovered oil in secondary and tertiary oil recovery processes

Companies that stand to benefit directly from genetic engineering are:

Biogen
Cetus
Genentech

Companies that may benefit indirectly are:

Bio-Rad Labs
Eli Lilly
Flow General
Monsanto
Schering-Plough, Inc.

Leading scientists conclude that understanding genetic makeup helps predict an individual's susceptibility to many diseases.

Open-Air sees further breakthroughs in the eighties. Major improvements in disease prevention and a more liberal attitude by the FDA make the health-care companies look attractive. In the hospital field, medical instrumentation is most interesting, as a result of the Reagan administration's seeking lower costs through increased competition. Earlier detection of cancer and improvement in detecting heart disease are other areas of advancement. Companies involved include:

American Home Products
Key Pharmaceuticals
Marion Laboratories
Merck
Pfizer
Schering-Plough
SmithKline Corp.

Of special interest are three areas also emerging as subgroups within the hospital/health-care category: providers of geriatric-care equipment (Lumex); providers of alcoholic treatment (Comprehensive Care); and providers of hospital patient delivery systems (HBO and Nadacom).

A modern, exotic offshoot of the biotechnology business might be monoclonal antibody research. A monoclonal antibody (MA) is an antibody cloned from a single cell. Antibodies are called the first line of defense in destroying foreign substances in the body. Monoclonal antibodies are frequently the reagents used by researchers in various types of cell sorting. Since these substances are purified and reproducible, they have tremendous promise as diagnostic tools. They can be aimed at specific targets in the body. Numerous companies are now manufacturing or will be producing diagnostic kits that will work on the MA principle, perhaps in early detection of cancer. Companies involved in this area are:

Becton Dickinson
Cetus
Damon Corporation
Hybritech
Monoclonal Antibodies
New England Nuclear Division of Du Pont
Ortho Drug Division of Johnson & Johnson

Robots as a breakthrough? Invest in R2D2? Robots are here to stay. They weld, they test, and they don't need coffee breaks, grievance committees, or two-martini lunches. According to *Barron's*, this industry could be $500 million by 1985, but the trade association, The Robot Institute of America, projects a more conservative $214 million. Auto companies are now the biggest customers. Robots contain computer memories so they can be programmed for various jobs. Leading companies in this field are:

Cincinnati Milacron
Condec
Ransburg Corporation

Dick Tracy has come of age in the eighties. Mobile phones will be a big, big deal. Remember the two-way wrist radio? It's called a cellular phone, and American Telephone was given an okay by the FCC to retain one-half of the available radio frequency space in every market for use by the cellular subsidiary of the local phone company. Other competitors of AT&T will fight over the other half—which is enormous. The word *cellular* comes about because a city is divided into cells, each served by its own transmitter. Computers automatically pass a caller from one cell, or frequency, to another as one moves through the city in one's car. A wife driving home from work can call her husband and have him pick up something at the store. Or she can "beep" him on the golf course. Call your broker while driving down the street. Will a businessman need an office? "We're talking about a revolution in lifestyle," says a spokesman from Motorola. Companies in this field are:

American Telephone
Communications Industries
E. F. Johnson
Graphic Scanning
Motorola
Radiofone

It is important to digress here a minute. All of these are not stock tips! They are exposed as possible areas for Open-Air Analysis, fundamental analysis, technical analysis, and all the other analyses you must do with your broker once you first observe the obvious. Furthermore, Du Pont can make a breakthrough in gene splicing, and it will not have the impact on a multibillion-dollar sales base that a breakthrough by Genentech will have on a $10 million sales base. Hence, there is greater likelihood of a company with a smaller sales base having its earnings increase dramatically and also its price-to-earnings ratio.

Remember Henrietta Headline? She always listened to the evening news and read the morning paper. "The evening news says we're heading into a recession; the morning paper says inflation is heating up; and three economists on *Face the Nation* said we are losing out to foreign competition . . . blah, blah, blah." By the time the economists are calling a turn, the stock market has already forecast it. The stock market has a far better record of forecasting than do economists. As previously described, they are like six people sleeping in one bed—when one rolls over the others will. The economists did break with tradition, as this February 1981 article from *The Wall Street Journal* indicates:

> Most economists don't seem to agree with Joseph Granville about prospects for the stock market.
>
> Mr. Granville's famous warning to his many clients last month to "sell everything" was widely blamed for a single-day drop of some 24 points in the Dow Jones industrial average. He remains pessimistic, and it's a fact that the average has fallen further in recent weeks. It closed yesterday at 942.49.
>
> Unlike Mr. Granville, economists tend to shy away from stock market predictions. They no doubt have enough trouble forecasting such things as gross national product. But they do occasionally let their views on the market be known, usually on a no-names basis. Robert Eggert's latest survey of leading economists contains a stock market section. It shows that, on the average, they expect the

Dow Jones average to reach 990 within six months, 1080 in a year, and 1145 in 18 months.

The group also rates oil-field services and equipment as the "best" share category, with drug stocks a distant second. The "worst" rating goes to savings-and-loan shares, with auto makers right behind.

But they did it again! Notice they rated oil-field services as best, and savings and loans and autos as worst. Interestingly enough, two of the worst performing groups in January, February, and March of 1981 were oils and oil services, and as for autos, General Motors climbed over 25% in the three months of January, February, and March 1981. Remember what Schwartz says, "Only take advice from people who have to live with that advice." Economists, journalists, analysts, advisory services, etc., don't know you and, least of all, can't be held accountable; your broker has to live with his recommendations. The economists were closer on the market, but they were in the wrong stocks. So, even if you spot an Open-Air dandy by keeping your eyes and ears open, you will always have plenty of reasons *not* to take action. Every good idea is born drowning in a sea of reasons why it won't work.

Back to making money. What are the problems of the eighties? Invest in water in the eighties—the price is going up. If energy was the problem in the seventies, then water will take its place in the eighties. And there's one big difference: there's no substitute for water. Maybe rooftops in the future will be designed like those in Bermuda to catch rain. Who makes pumps? Who makes reservoir equipment? Who makes water pipes? Will the oil drillers become water drillers?

There are two sources of water—rainfall and ground water (aquifers). Both of these sources might be threatened in the eighties. Aquifers are being depleted at accelerating rates. The ground above these aquifers is generally difficult to penetrate, so new rainfall cannot replenish the water lost. And rainfall is not dependable. In a February 1981 *Newsweek* article, it was stated:

> Even in the driest years, rain across the country enormously exceeds water use. The trouble is that the nation's water resources are badly out of balance. The Northwest has a big surplus, for example, while the agriculture states of the Southwest scrape for the last salty dregs from the Colorado River.

Further, according to *Newsweek*, all water comes as rain from the sky, but 92% of it either evaporates immediately or runs off, unused, to the oceans. One quarter of the water that irrigates, powers, and bathes America is taken from an ancient network of underground aquifers. Each day 21 billion more gallons flow out than seep in. Already in January of 1981, the state of New York had declared a water emergency.

What are the investment possibilities? Metering of water could be a partial answer to the problem. Recycling water is another possibility. One company—PureCycle, of Boulder, Colorado—has developed a system for a homeowner to install, at a cost of $18,000, which will completely recycle all the waste water into drinking water.

What does this mean for food? Food is affected by less water, contaminated water, and less land to grow on. The water crisis could focus new attention on hydroponics—the growing of food without soil. Whittaker Corporation, Control Data, and General Mills are becoming involved in this. Another possible breakthrough is the use of genetic engineering to grow one plant from the cell of another. Monsanto is working in this field. Actually some experts predict cloning breakthroughs in food before medicine. According to *Forbes* magazine in a February 1981 article by Bob Tamarkin, the following chemical companies are all increasing their research and development in this effort:

Dow
Du Pont
Monsanto
Stouffer

Other companies involved in solving water problems are:

Betz	Ionics
Foster Wheeler	Millipore
General Signal	Nalco
Great Lakes Chemical	Pall
Wheelabrator Frye	

Another problem to invest in in the eighties is crime. It's 30 times earnings. Companies like Burns, Pinkerton, Detector Systems, Wackenhut, and ADT are heavily involved in security protection. Open-Air says you can spot the ADT symbol on the windows of business establishments. Budget cuts mean less money for police and fire protection, which involves a company like Wackenhut. Electronic surveillance is the James Bond approach to fighting crime. Other companies like Sensormatic, Knogo, and Universal Security Instruments are included.

Last, and perhaps the biggest, Open-Air says to watch China. Can you imagine Coca-Cola or Pepsi-Cola in China?

These are visible Open-Air possibilities now, but the climate can change. The practitioner is always looking, always reading, and always asking, "Who's the manufacturer?"

The false starts of the eighties might be solar energy, fusion, synfuels, and the electric car. Synfuel is already being de-emphasized as largely a boondoggle. In the seventies one of the continuing false starts was coal. Open-Air could have been deceived several times on this one. With respect to solar energy, the possible exception could be Ametek, which was issued a patent in the spring of 1981 on a solar photovoltaic device to convert light directly into electricity. Ametek's breakthrough came as a result of producing a low-cost simple process. The secret was using cadmium and tellurium rather than silicon.

Schwartz: Mark this day down in history: January 20, 1981. Reagan was sworn in, the hostages were released, and the market was down 20.

Broker: No real specifics in Reagan's address. Here's an interesting fact for you: the market closed about 30 points below where it was when Carter took office.

Schwartz: The Fed is still crunching. Hell, why not? They finally have a president who understands and appreciates the function of the Fed.

Broker: What does Open-Air see to make money as a result of Reagan's supply-side economics?

Schwartz: Same deal. We're in them: foods, consumer issues, at long last. It's obvious! If you disinflate, the dollar gets stronger. If the dollar gets stronger, the consumer starts to have confidence in buying basics again.

Broker: Well, it's starting to happen. The market drops 60 or 70 points, and incoming calls dry up. The only calls are about our money market fund.

Schwartz: You're not a broker, you're...

Broker: A teller! "What are money markets paying?" is my biggest question.

Schwartz: The most obvious thing in this market is the weakness in oils and the strength in the things that consume oil. In fact, Knogo reported a

	down earning quarter. Let's sell it and buy Eastern Air Lines.
Broker:	Airlines consume oil and are acting suspiciously strong. Our firm feels Eastern will earn $1.50 this year and maybe $3.00 in '82. Do you want the common or the warrants? The warrants are convertible at ten and have another seven years till expiration. They are 2⅞.
Schwartz:	Let's get the warrants.
Broker:	Okay. We sold 1,000 Knogo at 17 and bought 5,000 Eastern Air Lines warrants at 2⅞. Profit on Knogo was $3,375. I hate to say it, but the only stock you own 100 shares of has doubled.
Schwartz:	The garbage stock, Waste Management? You didn't like Minnetonka at first, and I didn't really like Waste Management. So, I always like that situation to complain about. By the way, how the hell are you doing in all this? You know how your clients are doing, but we don't know how you're doing.
Broker:	I'm in all the same Open-Airs that you are, only in a smaller way. The Open-Air club is getting rich, also.
Schwartz:	Open-Air club?
Broker:	Yes. I've got about fifteen or twenty clients that are all Open-Air members. Some ideas are coming from you, some from me, and some from them.
Schwartz:	I'll be damned—a capitalistic commune.
Broker:	You've got it. Share the wealth. Just keep praying that Joe Granville and Henry Kaufman keep up their act and drive this market down, because we're picking up some cheap stock in here.

"They are peaking."

(The next month)

Schwartz: Do you think the 920-930 will hold again?

Broker: Yes. This market is saddled; the jocks are up and parading to the post; and all we're doing is walking around behind the gate. This is the race called "break the old all-time high." The horse called Stock Market wants to be last to load in the gate. He's waiting for Spending Cuts, Interest Rates, Commodity Prices, and Congressional Reaction to load. Then he will walk in, and the race to 1,050 will be on.

Schwartz: If he doesn't fall on his face coming out of the gate.

Broker: No, the pieces are falling into place; Reagan means business. In fact, mark this day down, Schwartz, February 25, 1981, as a major turning point.

Schwartz: You sound like Granville.
Broker: Seriously, the market at one time today was down 11 and finished up 8. Of more importance, while it was down 11, GM, Eastman Kodak, and Du Pont were all up.
Schwartz: Are you still a teller? Still answering incoming questions about money market funds?
Broker: My first team and all Open-Air members are *buying*. Everyone else asks about T-bills and money market rates. I can't get them to do anything.
Schwartz: Oh, yes, all good Open-Air signs. When the incoming calls get so that your secretary has to put me on hold several days in a row, then I'll know...
Broker: It's time to lighten up a little.
Schwartz: You know, everybody maligns the stock market, but it's the only place I know where I can raise money in a hurry. Speaking of raising money, I'm close to selling Minnetonka. Two of the stores I go to on field trips said Softsoap is slowing down a little—more competition. Dammit, I wish I were long-term!
Broker: Well, if it isn't Larry Long-Term. Anyway, the strength in the market is obvious.
Schwartz: I agree. I think we're going through 1,000, but then what's obvious to you and me might not be obvious to others.
Broker: That's the difference between Open-Air pros and Open-Air rookies. The pro sees things sooner. I bet a guy we would be through 1,000 by Easter. Schwartz, going into early March, my gross is down, but this thing is going to explode.
Schwartz: What turned you on?

Broker:	I'm still a teller. I have a client with 300 Ashland Oil. It's up 8 points in two days, and she was complaining about a 60¢ discrepancy in her dividend—never mentioned her Ashland. And still no incoming calls.
Schwartz:	The public is doing it again. Money market funds are going down, stocks are going up, and people are going into money market funds—the things that are going down.
Broker:	London market is now back over 500. This is supposed to be a March 1981 massacre according to Granville.
Schwartz:	Well, we got over 1,000 the first time on March 16, 1981, on 50 million shares, but only 129 new highs. That's not too persuasive.
Broker:	Always bitching. And your stocks were well represented in that new high list.
Schwartz:	I know ... I know.

(The next week)

Broker:	Well, we went over 1,000 again on March 23 on 58 million shares and 175 new highs. I think the 1,000 that was the ceiling of the seventies will become the floor of the eighties.
Schwartz:	It's turning into a real March massacre for the shorts. Just like Granville said, only in reverse.
Broker:	But we still get bashful at the 1,000 level. Yesterday, we were at 1,015 and finished at 997.
Schwartz:	Forget the market. All I see are pregnant women, and Gerber keeps making new highs. This damn 1,000 area distracts me from Open-Air. What am I doing with only 500 Gerber?
Broker:	Hell, your broker owns more than you do. I own 1,500.

Schwartz: Keep that up and you can be a client too, someday. And your other clients? How are they doing?

Broker: Schwartz, you're the leader of a cult. Without revealing names, Open-Air has made about fifteen of us rich.

Schwartz: Us?

Broker: I told you in the beginning I planned to make a mil. Meeting you was my ticket, and those others have become believers.

Schwartz: Well, I'm up this last year over 65%, so I'm approaching $400,000.

Broker: My game plan is to stay within half of you.

Schwartz: But you know my portfolio, and I really don't know yours.

Broker: Sure you do, I always tell you. I had most of them except Minnetonka—the biggie. Those fifteen Open-Air clients have done well also. Oh, I forgot, Minnetonka is having a secondary. Not the best sign in the world.

(A few days later)

Broker: They shot Reagan.

Schwartz: Let's buy Wackenhut, Pinkerton, Burns, and ADT.

Broker: No, I'm serious.

Schwartz: So am I!

Broker: Open-Air to the end.

Schwartz: Crime is 30 times earnings.

Broker: Well, we can't do anything now because they just suspended trading.

Schwartz: I hope to God he's all right, but even if it's bad, remember the Monday following the Friday assassination of Kennedy?

Broker: The market was up substantially and, in fact, rose for about four years.

(A few days later)

Broker: Reagan's okay, and the market's up 11, back above 1,000 on 51 million. Anticrime stocks are all strong.

Schwartz: Open-Air says buy them! Do I have any buying power?

Broker: Not unless you want to go right to the limit.

Schwartz: No, and I don't really want to sell anything either, so we become spectators on this one.

Broker: It's been a hell of a year: Bunker Hunt, hostages, highest prime rate in history, Afghanistan, a new president, Granville, and now this. Can you believe I put some clients into A rated tax-free bonds today with a 12% yield?

Schwartz: Crazy, but Open-Air never let us down. We made the usual mistakes—only owning 100 Waste Management, that damn thing is over 100. We never bought the soccer stock, AMF, and it's up 40%.

Broker: Plus we sold Sears and Ford at losses, and they're up, but so are the stocks we bought with the proceeds. For instance, your GM is up almost 10 points. And it was just announced that the FDA has approved Capoten, so Squibb has turned strong. But you sold that.

Schwartz: '82 and '83 will be the years for the American car. You'd think everyone would be buying GM and Ford with the administration putting the pressure on the Japanese.

Broker: And relaxing controls over the auto industry.

Schwartz: And Tony Lama went up after we sold it, but

then look at how those oils cratered after we sold, so it all evens up. Did you get most of your clients out of oils?

Broker: All that I could. But you know, you call some people and advise them to sell Exxon or Gulf, and they think you're after a commission. A blue chip like Gulf Oil has fallen from 52 to 32 in a little over three months. How's this for a quick change in direction: at the end of the year, Delta Airlines, which consumes oil, was at 59 and as of today, April 14, it's 73½. Standard of Ohio in the same period has gone from 72 to 45⅜.

Schwartz: People are funny about labels. In the final analysis, a blue-chip stock is one that's going up. Remember my old Brunswick bowling observation, "Now I can find an alley"? Well, now I can find plenty of oil. It might tighten up later, but oils won't see those old highs for a while.

Broker: The agony of the holding period and the ecstacy of the profit period. People have problems with stocks at different levels. Some can't stand it if it does nothing for two months. Others are skeptical all the way up and then, when it doubles or triples, it's a blue chip and should not be sold. It's a big transition, a world glut of oil easily seen by Open-Air—but try and get people out of Standard Oil of California.

Schwartz: Speaking of future blue chips, I did one of my Open-Air field trips, which included an interesting conversation with a fellow airplane passenger.

Broker: Yes-s-s?

Schwartz: And if I haven't uncovered what might be my biggest winner, then my name's not . . .

Broker: 100% Schwartz. I'm listening—because when Schwartz talks, people listen...

Schwartz: First, I've found a new industry. Second, I've zeroed in on a couple of companies that will... well, what if I told you... look, you're going to die when I tell you because it's so obvious...

INDEX

Abelson, Alan, 24, 176
ADT, 201
Advisory services, 82, 149–50.
  See also Granville, Joe
Airlines, 203
Alcan Aluminum, 52, 136
Alpha Industries, 41
Amerada Hess, 136
American Airlines, 39
American Brands, 41, 53, 136
American Express, 193
American Home Products, 195
American Medical International, 33, 136
American Stock Exchange Index, 18
American Telephone & Telegraph, 45, 113, 114, 191–92, 197
Ametek, 202
AMF, 11, 168
Ampex, 136
Analog Devices, 53
Analysis, stock, 8
Antibodies, monoclonal, 196
Apple Computer, 84, 104, 191
Applicon, 84, 171, 193
Armour, 38, 49
ASA, 42
ATO, 168

AT&T. *See* American Telephone & Telegraph
Atwood Oceanics, 136
Auto industry, 190, 208
Automatic teller, 3, 180
Auto Train, 161
Auto-trol Technology, 137, 193
Avon, 39
Aydin Corporation, 136

Bache, 137
Baker International, 137
Bally Manufacturing, 34
BanCal Tri-State, 143
BancTec, 84
Bard (C.R.) Inc., 53
Barron's, 24, 37, 189, 196
Barry Wright, 59, 60, 137
Baruch, Bernard, 118
Bausch & Lomb, 35, 52, 137
Bear market, 117
Becton Dickinson, 196
Belco Petroleum, 137
Beldridge Oil, 151
Benguet, 42
Betz, 201
Beverly Enterprises, 33, 137
Biogen, 195
Bio-Rad Labs, 195

Biotechnology industry, 194, 196, 200–201
"Bo Dereks," 15, 24
Boeing, 18
Bonds, 24, 55
Borden, 183, 190
Bottom, stock market, 13, 19, 23, 29–30
Bowling, 9–11
Bow Valley Industries, 137
Breakthroughs, 34, 194–98
Brokerage firms, 75–76, 85–86, 87, 89
  stocks of, 48, 180
Brokers, 66–75
  commissions, 77–82
  competition among, 81–82
  complaints about, 72
  dealing with, 100–103, 132–34
  discount, 86–88, 92
  earnings of, 80
  evaluating, 128–36
  friendships with, 101
  gifts to, 97–98
  Open-Air Analysis and, 93
  personal accounts of, 84, 133–34
  selecting, 85–86, 117
  services of, 82–83, 89
  types of, 72–75
  See also Brokerage firms
Brunswick, 9–11
Bull market, 117
Bunker Hunt day, 13–18, 25, 136
Burns, 201
Business Week, 37, 173, 184
Buttes Gas and Oil, 137

Cabot Corporation, 137
CAD/CAM industry, 193
Caesars World, 34, 38
Campbell Red Lake, 42, 137
Capoten, 154, 208
CBS, 191
Cellular telephone, 113–14, 197
Cenco, 137
Cenvill Communities, 42
Cessna Aircraft, 39
Cetus, 195, 196

Chieftain Development, 42
Chris-Craft, 42
Christiana Companies, 42
Church's Fried Chicken, 39
Cincinnati Milacron, 42, 197
Cities Service, 179
City Investing, 42, 137
Clients, rules for, 98–103
Coal, 38, 201
Coastal States Gas, 42
Coldwell Banker, 36, 48
Collins Foods, 40
Commission-free offerings, 83–84
Commissions, brokers', 77–82, 87, 88–89
Commodities, 70–71, 173, 190
Commodore International, 42, 43–44, 54, 104, 137, 191
Communications Industries (company), 197
Communications industry, 113–14, 197. *See also* Telecommunications industry
Comprehensive Care, 196
Computer industry, 37, 43–44, 104–105, 191, 192–93
Computervision, 43–44, 54, 59–60, 137, 193
Condec, 197
Consolidated Foods, 35, 190
Contact lenses, 35
Continental Telephone, 192
Contrarians, 27, 50
Control Data, 137, 200
Cooper Tire and Rubber, 126–27, 171
Country-and-western craze, 30
Cox Broadcasting, 52
CPT, 193
Crime industry, 201
Crock-Pot, 35–36, 41

Damon Corporation, 196
Datapoint, 137
Day-care centers, 191
Dayco, 40
Dean Witter Reynolds, 75, 137
Delhi International Oil, 42
Delta Airlines, 40

Delux Check, 52
Demography, 32–33, 173–74, 190–91
Denelcor, 137
Detector Systems, 201
Diebold, 3
Digital Equipment, 59, 60
Discount brokers, 86–88, 92
Disinflation, 173, 189–90, 193, 202
Diversification, 159
Dividends, 54–55, 115
Dome Mines, 42, 137
Dome Petroleum, 42, 161
Donahue Show, 177
Dow Chemical, 201
Dow Jones averages, 128, 175, 181, 194
Down markets, 18–19, 55–57, 75, 78, 135–36. *See also* Bunker Hunt day
Drug industry. *See* Health care industry
Dun and Bradstreet, 193
Du Pont, 196, 201

Earnings, of companies, 45, 53, 115
Eastern Airlines, 203
Eastman Kodak, 18, 31, 58–59, 137, 171
Economists, 198–99
Eggert, Robert, 198
Elia, Charles J., 176
Energy industry, 28–29, 33, 188–89. *See also* Oil
Engelhard Mineral, 42
Envirotech, 40
Enzo Biochem, 84
Equity Funding, 38
Equity funds, pooled, 128, 179, 181
Equity, on margin, 166–67
Error rate of brokerage firms, 88
Esterline Corporation, 42, 137
Exxon, 28, 137

Fads, 132–33
Falling markets. *See* Down markets
Fear, and the investor, 30, 116
Fiber-optics industry, 47
Firestone, 41, 58, 59
First Mississippi, 42
First Pennsylvania Bank, 25
First team, 84, 141–43, 148–49
Fleetwood, 161
Flight Safety International, 42
Florida Steel, 137
Flow General, 137, 195
Fluke (John), 137
Fluor, 42
Food industry, 173, 183, 184, 190, 200–201
Forbes magazine, 37, 176, 200–201
Ford, 40, 58–59, 152–53, 169–70, 190
Forecasts, 198
Fortune, 37
Foster Wheeler, 201
Fotomat, 40
Freeport Minerals, 137
Frozen accounts, 147
Fusion, 201

Gambling stocks, 34
Gasoline supply, 36, 161, 169–70, 183. *See also* Oil
GCA, 42, 137
Genentech, 84, 125–26, 194–95
General Defense, 84
General Electric, 191, 194
General Mills, 184, 190, 200
General Motors
 on Bunker Hunt day, 18
 candidate for breakup, 191–92
 and dividends, 55
 hard to sell, 171–72
 January 7, 1981, 177
 1978–80 performance, 40
 1980s prediction for, 190
 oil supply and, 153
General Public Utilities, 38, 40
General Signal, 201
Genetic engineering, 194–95, 200–201
Georgia Pacific, 190
Geosource, 42, 137

Gerber, 153–54, 171, 190, 191
Gerber Scientific, 42, 43, 44, 137, 193
Getty, 179
Giddings & Lewis, 52
Gillette, 137
GK Technology, 42
Global Marine, 42, 137
Goodyear, 40, 58–59, 137, 183, 190
Granville, Joe, 24, 175–78, 198
Graphic Scanning, 45, 113–14, 192, 197
Great Lakes Chemical, 201
Greed, and the investor, 96–97, 99, 116
Greyhound Corporation, 38, 49
Gulf Canada Ltd., 161
Gulf Oil, 7, 18
Gulf & Western, 52

Halliburton, 28
Hanes, 35
Hart Schaffner & Marx, 173–74
HBO, 196
Health care industry, 33, 195–96
Heath, 104
Helmerich & Payne, 42
Hershey, 190
Hitschler, Anthony, 179
Hospital Corporation of America, 33, 52, 138
Hospital industry, 33, 195–96
Housing industry, 29, 36, 190
Hudson's Bay Oil and Gas, 153
Hughes Tool, 28, 33, 138
Humana, 33, 52, 59, 60, 138
Hunt, Nelson Bunker, 16, 24–25, 90. *See also* Bunker Hunt day
Hutton, E. F., 42, 75, 87, 138
Hybritech, 196

IBM, 18, 58–59, 191–92, 193
Inflation, 185, 189. *See also* Disinflation
Information vending, 192–93
Intel, 138
Intercity Gas, 18, 161
Interconnect industry, 192

Interest rates
 bonds and utilities and, 55
 declining, effect of, 23–24
 explanation of, 21
 on margin, 165
 March 1980, 15
 November 1980, 175
 1981 prediction, 184–85
Interferon, 194
Intergraph, 193
Intermark, 138
International Business Machines. *See* IBM
Institutional money managers, 178–81
Insurance of stock market accounts, 164
Investors, types of, 4–5, 108–14
Investors Intelligence, 150
Ionics, 201
ISC Systems, 54, 84, 180, 193
Itek, 40
Itel, 17, 37, 40, 161

Jim Walter, 138
Johnson, E. F., 113, 114, 197
Johnson & Johnson, 155, 171, 196
Juniper, 28, 29, 170

Kaufman, Henry, 126, 175, 177
Kaufman & Broad, 190
Kenilworth Realty, 53
Key Pharmaceuticals, 195
Kimberly-Clark, 155, 168
Kirby Explorations, 138
K Mart, 40
Knogo, 30, 31, 170, 201
Kodak. *See* Eastman Kodak

Late payments, 147
Legal clinics, 191
Lennar, 138, 190
Levitz, 191
Lifemark, 33, 138
Lilly, Eli, 195
Limit orders, 115
Logicon, 138
Long-term investors, 116
Loral, 52

Losers, traits of, 108, 115–23
Lubrizol Corporation, 53
Lumex, 196

MA/COM, 47, 52, 54, 71, 138, 171
Macy, 53
Magazines, recommended for investors, 37
Magic Chef, 191
Magma Power, 42, 138
Magnuson Computer, 84, 170
Managing your portfolio, 51, 53–60, 99, 157–67
Margin accounts, 13, 19, 122, 164–67
Marion Laboratories, 195
Mark Products, 54
Mary Kay, 53, 138
Massey Ferguson, 40
Mattel, 138
MCA, 104, 191
McGraw-Hill, 53
MCI Communications, 45, 46–47, 54, 138, 171, 192
Memorex, 40, 157–58
Merck, 195
Merrill Lynch, 59, 60, 75, 87, 138
Mesa Petroleum, 52, 138
MGM, 191
MicomSystems, 192
Microwave Associates. *See* MA/COM
Microwave industry. *See* Telecommunications industry
Millipore, 201
Minnetonka, 63, 71, 126, 171
Mitchell Energy & Development, 42, 138
Mobile telephone, 113–14, 197
Mobil Oil, 18, 28
Mohawk Data Science, 138
Money supply, 61
Monoclonal antibodies, 196
Monsanto, 195, 200–201
Mortgage rates, 21
Motorola, 113, 197
Murphy Oil, 53
Mutual funds, 179, 181

Nabisco, 183, 184, 190
Nadacom, 196
Nalco, 201
Napco, 53
National Medical Enterprises, 33, 52, 138
NBI, 193
Network Systems, 193
New England Nuclear Division of Du Pont, 196
Newhall Land, 53
New issues, 83–84
Newspapers, recommended for investors, 37
Newsweek, 200
New York Times, The, 26, 37, 193
Nicolet Instruments, 138
NL Industries, 43
North American Philips, 104
Nucor, 43, 138
Nursing-home stocks, 33

Oak Industries, 8, 138, 191
Oil
  consumers of, 202–203
  industry, 28–29, 153
  service companies, 33
  stocks, 7, 36, 169–70, 179, 182–83, 209
  supply, 124, 161, 188–89
One-eighth rule, 123–24
Open-Air Analysis
  broker and, 93
  definition, 3–4, 8
  how to develop, 37–38
  how it works, 32
  prerequisites of, 5
  for selling stocks, 38–40
Options, 54, 70, 115
Ortho Drug Division of Johnson & Johnson, 196
Outboard Marine, 40
Overseas Shipholding, 53
Oversubscribed offerings, 83, 84
Overthrust, 29

Pacific Scientific, 138
Pall, 201
Palm Beach, 138

Panic, and the investor, 65, 161.
    See also Bunker Hunt day
Paradyne, 43, 138
Personalities of investors, 107–14
Petro Lewis, 43, 54, 138, 153, 176
Pfizer, 195
Pinkerton, 201
Pioneer Corporation, 43
Polaroid, 58, 59
Politics and the stock market, 90, 111
Pooled equity funds, 128, 181
Portfolio management, 51, 53–60, 99, 157–67
Portfolio reviews, 82–83, 130–31, 164
Predictions
    Joe Granville and, 175–78
    of 1980s trends, 188–93
Preppy look, 93–94
Prime Computer, 138, 176
Prime rate, 21
Problems, Open-Air Analysis and, 32, 199–201
Procter & Gamble, 154–55
Professional Tape Reader, 150
PureCycle, 200

Quaker Oats, 190

Radiofone, 113, 192, 197
Radio paging, 113–14
Radio Shack, 8
Ransburg Corporation, 197
Rather, Dan, 176
Ratings, 43
RCA, 104, 191
Reading & Bates, 33, 138
Real estate, 14, 27, 36, 48, 189
Recognition Equipment, 139
Recreational vehicles, 161
Redman, 161
Regan, Donald T., 15
Reneging, 146–47
Researching a company, 56–57
Resorts International-A, 34
Return, rates of, 128, 181
Rival Manufacturing, 35–36
Robots, 196–97

Rogers, Will, 95
Rolm, 43–45, 54, 59–60, 71, 139, 192
Rookie brokers, 79
Royal Dutch, 179
Ruff, Howard, 27, 150
Rules for clients, 98–103

Safety-Kleen, 180
Salomon Brothers High-Grade Bond Index, 128, 181
Sambo's Restaurants, 40, 41
Samuelson, Paul A., 150
Santa Fe International, 29, 33, 139
Schering-Plough, Inc., 195
Schlumberger, 28, 33
Schwartz, 100%, 9–12, 26–31, 46–48, 60–72, 89–94, 103–106, 123–27, 148–56, 167–74, 182–85, 202–10
Scientific Atlanta, 53, 59, 60, 139
SCOA, 53
Sears, 40, 45, 58–59, 92, 169
Secondary issues, 83
Second team, 142
Securities Investor Protection Corporation, 82, 164
Sedco, 43, 52
SEI, 193
Selling stocks, timing for, 45, 108–109
Seminars, investment, 27
Sensormatic, 30, 31, 170, 201
Service Fracturing, 84
Shearson American Express (Shearson Loeb Rhoades) 18, 43, 48, 54, 75, 139, 171
Sheller-Globe, 40
Silver market, 25, 31. *See also* Hunt, Nelson Bunker
Singer Co., 39
Singer, S. Fred, 188
Singleton, Henry, 54
SIPC, 82, 164
Skirt lengths, 113
SmithKline Corporation, 36, 195
Soccer, 168
Softsoap, 63–64, 71, 126
Solar energy, 201, 202

INDEX

Southern Pacific, 45, 192
Speculating, 29, 32
Sperry Top Siders, 94
Splits, 164
Squibb, 154, 208
Staley, A. E., 43
Standard Oil of California, 7, 43
Standard Oil of Indiana, 7, 28–29, 43, 52, 170, 177
Standard Oil of Ohio, 29, 170, 177
Standard & Poor's 500, 128, 181
Stanley Works, 53
Statements, monthly, 130–31, 164
Stauffer Chemical, 40
Stillwell, Newcomb, 176
Stockbrokerage stocks, 48, 180
Stockbrokers. *See* Brokers
Stock market
  and forecasting, 198
  influence on winners and losers, 116
  managing your position, 55–57, 117
  and politics, 90, 111
  predicted boom, 48
  signs of top and bottom, 13, 119, 122
  See also Down markets
Stocks
  managing, 51, 53–60
  when to buy, 51
  when to sell, 45, 108–109
  vs. the stock market, 57
Stone & Webster, 53
Stop-loss orders, 53, 115
Stouffer Foods, 4, 201
Street name accounts, 82, 131, 163–64
Stride Rite, 93–94
Subject offerings, 83–84
Sunbeam, 191
Sun Belt, 61
Swanson, Robert, 126
Synfuels, 29, 201

Tamarkin, Bob, 201
Tandy Corporation, 8, 54, 104, 139, 191

Technicolor, 43, 52
Telecom Equipment, 192
Telecommunications (company), 192
Telecommunications industry, 8, 44–47, 103–105, 191–93, 197
Teledyne, 8, 54, 59–60, 139
Telephone, mobile, 113–14, 197
Television, 8, 103–104, 191. *See also* Telecommunications industry
Teller, automatic, 3, 180
Tender offers, 164
Test, winners or losers, 115–23
Texaco, 7, 179
Texas International, 139
Texas Oil and Gas, 43
Third team, 148
Three Mile Island, 38, 40
Tidewater, 43
TIE Communications, 45, 139, 192
Tiffany & Co., 25–26
TII Industries, 192
Tipperary, 153
Tom Brown, 7, 54, 139
Tony Lama, 30–31, 171, 173
Topaz, 139
Towner Petroleum, 139
Toxic shock syndrome, 154–55
Treasury bills, 15, 21, 24
Trends, in 1980s, 188–93
Triangle Pacific, 40
Twentieth Century-Fox, 36
Tyler Corporation, 40

Union Oil, 179
Universal Communication System, 192
Universal Security Instruments, 201
Upjohn, 52, 139
U.S. Home, 43, 190
U.S. Plywood, 190
U. S. Steel, 40, 58, 59
Utilities, 55, 83

Valtec, 139
Veeco Instruments, 139

Viacom International, 43
Video disc, 104, 191
Volcker, Paul A., 184–85

Wackenhut, 201
Wainoco, 18, 28, 43, 59, 60, 139
Wall Street Journal, The, 37, 188, 198–99
Wang Laboratories, 36, 43, 44, 193
Warner Communications, 52
Waste Management, 43, 53, 94, 139, 171
Water supply, 199–201
Webb Corporation, Del, 40
Western Airlines, 40

Western Company of North America, 139
Western Union, 192
Wheelabrator Frye, 201
White Motor Company, 40, 161
Whittaker Corporation, 200
Winnebago, 161
Winners or losers test, 115–23
Winning investors, 4–5
Word processing industry, 44, 193
Wyle Labs, 53

Zapata, 33
Zenith, 103–105, 120, 139, 171, 191
Zentec, 193